T0154045

Ælfric of Eynsham.

Medieval Institute Publications is a program of
The Medieval Institute, College of Arts and Sciences

 WESTERN MICHIGAN UNIVERSITY

Ælfric of Eynsham

His Life, Times,
and Writings

Helmut Gneuss

Old English Newsletter Subsidia • 34

MEDIEVAL INSTITUTE PUBLICATIONS
Western Michigan University
Kalamazoo

© 2009 by the Board of Trustees of Western Michigan University
Printed and bound by CPI Group (UK) Ltd, Croydon, CR0 4YY
This book is printed on acid-free paper.

Library of Congress Cataloging-in-Publication Data

Gneuss, Helmut.
  [Ælfric von Eynsham und seine Zeit. English]
  Ælfric of Eynsham : his life, times, and writings / Helmut Gneuss.
    p. cm. – (Old English newsletter. Subsidia ; 34)
  Includes bibliographical references and index.
  ISBN 978-1-58044-144-5 (pbk. : acid-free paper)
  1. Aelfric, Abbot of Eynsham. I. Title.
  PR1534.G613 2008
  829–dc22
                                        2008039777

P   5   4   3   2   1

Originally published as *Ælfric von Eynsham und seine Zeit*
© 2002 by Bayerische Akademie der Wissenschaften

CONTENTS

PREFACE

This little book began as a lecture, delivered in German at a session of the Philosophisch-historische Klasse of the Bayerische Akademie der Wissenschaften in November 2000; it was subsequently published under the title *Ælfric von Eynsham und seine Zeit* in the *Sitzungsberichte* of the Class as Heft 1 in 2002. It had always been clear to me that the circulation in English-speaking countries of the German version would be limited, and it came, therefore, as a pleasant surprise and as an encouragement when, in December 2006, Paul Szarmach asked in a letter whether I had ever thought of an English version, which he might publish as a volume of the *Old English Newsletter Subsidia* series.

There was then some delay until, again unexpectedly, Michael Lapidge generously offered to translate text and notes into English—an offer more fortunate than I could ever have hoped for, coming from a great Anglo-Saxonist, and one who is perfectly familiar with Modern German. To him I owe this excellent English version of the original as well as valuable suggestions for improvement. Mechthild Gretsch also kindly contributed to contents and translation, in particular by clarifying a considerable number of German passages that turned out to be less lucid than I had imagined.

The text of this English version has essentially retained the substance and characteristics of the original, but the references in the footnotes have been updated as far as possible. These references must, of course, remain selective; there is a great deal of interesting work on Ælfric now available in print, recorded in the bibliographies cited in the first footnote.

I am grateful to Paul Szarmach, editor of the *Old English Newsletter Subsidia*, and Patricia Hollahan, managing editor of Medieval Institute Publications, Western Michigan University, for bringing out *þas lytlan boc* in their series. I wish to thank the Secretary General of the Bayerische Akademie der Wissenschaften, Mrs. Regenscheidt-Spies, for permission to produce and publish this English version.

Abbreviated References

ASE	*Anglo-Saxon England*
Blackwell Encyclopaedia	*The Blackwell Encyclopaedia of Anglo-Saxon England*, ed. Michael Lapidge, John Blair, Simon Keynes, and Donald Scragg (Oxford, 1999)
Catholic Homilies I	*Ælfric's Catholic Homilies: The First Series: Text*, ed. Peter Clemoes, EETS s.s. 17 (1997)
Catholic Homilies II	*Ælfric's Catholic Homilies: The Second Series: Text*, ed. Malcolm Godden, EETS s.s. 5 (1979)
Catholic Homilies III	*Ælfric's Catholic Homilies: Introduction, Commentary and Glossary*, by Malcolm Godden, EETS s.s. 18 (2000)
CSASE	Cambridge Studies in Anglo-Saxon England
EEMF	Early English Manuscripts in Facsimile
EETS o.s.	Early English Text Society, Original Series
EETS s.s.	Early English Text Society, Supplementary Series
Eynsham Letter	Christopher A. Jones, *Ælfric's Letter to the Monks of Eynsham*, CSASE 24 (Cambridge, 1998)
Grammatik	*Ælfrics Grammatik und Glossar. Text und Varianten*, ed. Julius Zupitza. 3rd ed. with a new introduction by Helmut Gneuss (Hildesheim, 2001; originally published Berlin, 1880)
Heptateuch	*The Old English Version of the Heptateuch, Ælfric's Treatise on the Old and New Testament and His Preface to Genesis*, ed. S. J. Crawford. With the text of two additional manuscripts transcribed by N. R. Ker, EETS o.s. 160 (1969; first published 1922). To be replaced by *The Old English Heptateuch and Ælfric's "Libellus de ueteri testamento et nouo,"* vol. 1, ed. Richard Marsden, EETS o.s. 330 (2008)
Hirtenbriefe	*Die Hirtenbriefe Ælfrics in altenglischer und lateinischer Fassung, mit Übersetzung und Einleitung*, ed. Bernhard Fehr. *Reprint with a Supplement to the Introduction* by Peter Clemoes, Bibliothek der

ix

	angelsächsischen Prosa IX (Darmstadt, 1966; first published Hamburg, 1914)
Homilies Suppl.	*Homilies of Ælfric: A Supplementary Collection, with Introduction, Notes, Latin Sources and a Glossary*, ed. John C. Pope, 2 vols., EETS o.s. 259, 260 (1967–68)
Keynes, *Bibliography*	Simon Keynes, *Anglo-Saxon England: A Bibliographical Handbook for Students of Anglo-Saxon History*, 7th ed. (Cambridge, 2006); cf. below, n. 1, on the publication history
Lapidge, *Library*	Michael Lapidge, *The Anglo-Saxon Library* (Oxford, 2006)
Lives of Saints	*Ælfric's Lives of Saints*, ed. Walter W. Skeat, EETS o.s. 76, 82, 94, 114 (1881–1900; repr. in two vols., 1966)
Reinsma	Luke M. Reinsma, *Ælfric: An Annotated Bibliography*, Garland Reference Library of the Humanities 617 (New York, 1987)
TUEPh	Texte und Untersuchungen zur Englischen Philologie (a series of publications of the University of Munich)
Vita Æthelwoldi	*Wulfstan of Winchester: The Life of St. Æthelwold*, ed. Michael Lapidge and Michael Winterbottom, Oxford Medieval Texts (Oxford, 1991); also includes an edition of Ælfric's *Vita S. Æthelwoldi* (pp. 70–80)
Wilcox, *Prefaces*	*Ælfric's Prefaces*, ed. Jonathan Wilcox, Durham Medieval Texts 9 (Durham, 1994)

Introduction

In this lecture I shall attempt to introduce an Anglo-Saxon author, one who does not, perhaps, shine as a star in the firmament as viewed by today's medievalists, but one who was the first, and for a long time the only, master of prose written in English. In what follows I mean to provide a sketch of Ælfric's life and work, but also of the historical background of his writings and their influence during the troubles which beset Anglo-Saxon England at the turn of the first millennium. Ælfric of Eynsham (for his epithet see below) was well known to students of the Anglo-Saxon period from the twelfth century, and particularly from the sixteenth century, onwards, and later also to the first students of English philology. But only in recent times have his most important writings become available in critical editions.[1] This, and other advances in research, among them the first inventory of everything preserved in manuscript from the Anglo-Saxon period,[2] permit a fresh assessment of the subject of the present study. It must also be said that, apart from a very small circle of specialists, Ælfric has hardly ever attracted scholarly attention, particularly on the Continent, where—outside the field of English studies—his importance has been appreciated by very few scholars (honorable exceptions here being Adolf Ebert and Max Manitius).[3]

1. Scholarly literature on Ælfric and his writings is listed, with very few omissions, by Luke M. Reinsma, *Ælfric: An Annotated Bibliography* (New York, 1987), continued selectively by Aaron Kleist, "An Annotated Bibliography of Ælfrician Studies: 1983–1996," in *Old English Prose: Basic Readings*, ed. Paul E. Szarmach (New York, 2000), pp. 503–52. For the period since 1983, see the annual bibliographies printed in *Anglo-Saxon England* and the *Old English Newsletter* (the cut-off date for Reinsma's bibliography was the end of 1982). Indispensable for the historical background (in the widest sense) is the bibliography, which has been updated and issued regularly since 1985, by Simon Keynes, *Anglo-Saxon England: A Bibliographical Handbook for Students of Anglo-Saxon History*, 7th ed. (Cambridge, 2006), 1st ed. 2000, preceded by fifteen editions (1985–99) under the title *Anglo-Saxon History: A Select Bibliography*.

2. Helmut Gneuss, *Handlist of Anglo-Saxon Manuscripts: A List of Manuscripts and Manuscript Fragments Written or Owned in England up to 1100*, Medieval and Renaissance Texts and Studies 241 (Tempe, AZ, 2001), with idem, "Addenda and Corrigenda to the *Handlist of Anglo-Saxon Manuscripts*," *ASE*, 32 (2003), 293–305; second addenda are in preparation. Michael Lapidge, *The Anglo-Saxon Library* (Oxford, 2006), provides an excellent analysis and history of library holdings. There are thorough descriptions of all manuscripts with Old English texts and glosses in N. R. Ker, *Catalogue of Manuscripts Containing Anglo-Saxon* (Oxford, 1957). For charters which are not listed in either of these books see Keynes, *Bibliography*, B 320–58.

3. Adolf Ebert, *Allgemeine Geschichte der Literatur des Mittelalters im Abendlande*, 2nd ed. (Leipzig, 1880–89), III. 509–16; Max Manitius, *Geschichte der lateinischen Literatur des Mittelalters*, II (Munich, 1923), pp. 676–82.

Ælfric's Name and Career

Astonishingly, seven centuries passed before anyone realized who Ælfric was. Even in the Middle Ages he was quickly forgotten. This is clear already from a poem dating probably from the end of the eleventh century, but recorded first in the thirteenth, in which it is lamented that the English people are no longer provided with religious teachings by speakers of their own language:

> Ælfric abbod, þe we Alquin hoteþ,
> he was bocare, and þe [fif] bec wende,
> Genesis, Exodus, Utronomius, Numerus, Leuiticus,
> þu[rh] þeos weren ilærde ure leoden on Englisc.[4]

Since the twelfth century Ælfric has been identified, wrongly, with various historically attested persons. William of Malmesbury, in every way an excellent student of Anglo-Saxon literature and history, took him to be an abbot of Malmesbury (965–77) who later became bishop of Crediton (977×979–985×987). Until well into the nineteenth century generally well informed antiquaries, historians, and philologists—among them John Leland, John Bale, Archbishop Parker, William Camden, Henry Spelman, Franciscus Junius, Henry Wharton, Jean Mabillon, Humfrey Wanley, as well as Elizabeth Elstob and Benjamin Thorpe—inclined to various different identifications: the prevailing opinion was that the great author of English prose was either Ælfric, archbishop of Canterbury (995–1005) and previously bishop of Ramsbury (991×993–995) and abbot of St. Albans (969–?990), or else Ælfric, archbishop of York (1023–51) and previously prior of the Old Minster in Winchester (or of the New Minster?).[5]

---

4. "Abbot Ælfric, whom we call Alcuin, he was a learned man, and translated the five books, Genesis, Exodus, Deuteronomy, Numbers, Leviticus; through these our people were taught in English." Worcester Cathedral, MS. F. 174, fol. 63; see S. K. Brehe, "Reassembling the First Worcester Fragment," *Speculum*, 65 (1990), 521–36, and Jones in *Eynsham Letter*, pp. 90–91; on the manuscript, see Ker, *Catalogue*, no. 398, and Christine Franzen, *The Tremulous Hand of Worcester: A Study of Old English in the Thirteenth Century* (Oxford, 1991), pp. 70–71 and passim, with a facsimile in pl. 10.

5. Reinsma, pp. 9-31, provides a survey of the early attempts (before Dietrich: see below, n. 7) at attribution of Ælfric's writings; but his survey requires the following amendments.

The explanation for this confusion is simple: it lies in the principle of Anglo-Saxon and Germanic personal naming. Alongside monothematic names the English, particularly those belonging to the upper classes, used dithematic names, that is, bipartite compounds, which were formed from a very limited number of elements. These functioned both as forenames and surnames; only occasionally was a byname added, with which personal characteristics (place of birth or residence, status, distinctive bodily features) could be designated. But a byname is by no means a surname. As a result, in our inevitably limited sources we often encounter substantial numbers of persons having the same name, a fact which even today poses serious problems for historical research. This pertains to the name Ælfric as well: in the early Anglo-Saxon period, up to the tenth century, the name appears to have been relatively uncommon, but for the tenth and eleventh centuries the older handbook of Anglo-Saxon personal names and persons—William George Searle's *Onomasticon Anglo-Saxonicum* (1897)—and the recently produced *Prosopography of Anglo-Saxon England* list more than one hundred persons named Ælfric, a striking number, even when one considers that two or more of those listed may be the same person. It is worth mentioning here that, for the period 940 to 1040 (the century in which the lifetime of Ælfric of Eynsham fell), there are twelve bishops or abbots with the name Ælfric.[6]

The first of the sixteenth-century antiquaries who wrote about Ælfric was not John Bale but John Leland (1506–52) in his *Commentarii de Scriptoribus Britannicis*, ed. Anthony Hall (Oxford, 1709), I. 169–70, cap. CXXXIII "De Ealfrico"; a new edition of the *Commentarii* by J. P. Carley is forthcoming (Toronto). Although Leland worked on these *Commentarii* (which were not published until much later) until 1545, this entry on Ælfric must date back to before the end of 1539. The entry by John Bale, *Scriptorum Illustrium Majoris Brytanniae Catalogus* (Basel, 1557–59), p. 149, is largely taken over from Leland. The article by Mabillon (reproduced in Migne PL 139, 1455–60: Reinsma no. 86) on Archbishop Ælfric of Canterbury derives from the *Acta Sanctorum Ordinis Sancti Benedicti* (Paris, 1668–1701), VIII. 55, and is not as uncritical as Reinsma implies, given that Mabillon was familiar with the works of Pits, Spelman, and Wharton. Humfrey Wanley unfortunately did not write his planned "Dissertation about Ælfric": cf. *Letters of Humfrey Wanley, Palaeographer, Anglo-Saxonist, Librarian, 1672–1726*, ed. P. L. Heyworth (Oxford, 1989), no. 83.—It would appear that a single contemporary refers to Ælfric by name, namely Ælfric Bata, who was probably his student; cf. below, n. 61.

6. There is exemplary treatment of Anglo-Saxon personal names, with references to scholarly literature, by Cecily Clark, "Onomastics," in *The Cambridge History of the English Language*, vol. 1: *The Beginnings to 1066*, ed. Richard M. Hogg (Cambridge, 1992), pp. 452–71 and 488. For persons having the name Ælfric, see William George Searle, *Onomasticon Anglo-Saxonicum* (Cambridge, 1897), pp. 16–19, and now "Ælfric 1"–"Ælfric 115" in *Prosopography of Anglo-Saxon England* <http:www.pase.ac.uk>, accessed 10 January 2008; also Simon Keynes, "Episcopal Succession in Anglo-Saxon England," in *Handbook of British Chronology*, ed. E. B. Fryde et al., 3rd ed. (Cambridge, 1986), pp. 209–24.

That we are today able to say with certainty who *our* Ælfric was, we owe to the Marburg theologian and philologist Franz Eduard Christoph Dietrich (1810–83), who in two learned and pioneering articles, published in the *Zeitschrift für die historische Theologie* for 1855 and 1856, laid the foundation for all subsequent research on our subject. This achievement was only possible because Dietrich had been able to familiarize himself with Ælfric's writings in manuscripts in English libraries—writings which at the time were still unpublished, or were available only in inadequate editions.[7]

However, a complete biography of Ælfric can no more be written today than it could at a previous time. We know the important stages of his life from short notices in the prefaces to some of his writings,[8] but much remains unclear. We do not know either the year of his birth or the year of his death, and know nothing of where he came from. In his early life he received instruction from a priest, whose knowledge of Latin was, according to Ælfric himself, defective.[9] From a sentence found in Ælfric's *Grammar*,

---

7. Eduard Dietrich, "Abt Aelfrik. Zur Literatur-Geschichte der angelsächsischen Kirche," *Zeitschrift für die historische Theologie*, 25 (1855), 487–594, and 26 (1856), 163–256. The pioneering contributions of this scholar to the developing awareness of Anglo-Saxon literature have unfortunately been largely forgotten; they are, however, listed in the extremely full and reliable handbook of Stanley B. Greenfield and Fred C. Robinson, *A Bibliography of Publications on Old English Literature to the End of 1972* (Toronto, 1980), cf. the index, p. 396. To Dietrich, for example, belongs the credit for first having recognized, and reported about, the leaf preserved in Kassel of the almost completely destroyed manuscript of King Alfred's version of the *Cura Pastoralis*, Cotton Tiberius B. xi, now Kassel, Gesamthochschulbibliothek 4° MS.theol. 131; to him, too, we owe the earliest notice of the Kentish dialect of Old English, cf. Ursula Kalbhen, *Kentische Glossen und kentischer Dialekt im Altenglischen*, TUEPh 28 (Frankfurt a.M., 2003), pp. 242–44. Some time passed before Dietrich's identification of our Ælfric became widely known and accepted, cf. for example Thomas D. Hardy, *Descriptive Catalogue of Materials Relating to the History of Great Britain and Ireland* (London, 1862–71), I. 586–87. Dietrich's research first became generally known through Walter W. Skeat in *Lives of Saints*, II. xxii–xxv, and Caroline Louisa White, *Ælfric: A New Study of His Life and Writings*, Yale Studies in English 2 (New York, 1898), reprinted with a supplementary classified bibliography by Malcolm R. Godden (Hamden, CT, 1974). Gunta Haenicke and Thomas Finkenstaedt, *Anglistenlexikon 1825–1990* (Augsburg, 1992), do not mention him. H. Reckendorf compiled a brief biography for the *Allgemeine Deutsche Biographie*, vol. 55 (Leipzig, 1910), pp. 733–34.

8. These have all been printed by Jonathan Wilcox, *Ælfric's Prefaces* (Durham, 1994). On Ælfric's life, see most recently Keynes, *Bibliography*, J 3.1; Godden in *Catholic Homilies*, III. xxix–xxxii; Wilcox, *Prefaces*, pp. 6–15; and Jones in *Eynsham Letter*, p. 5.

9. See Ælfric's preface to his version of Genesis, *Heptateuch*, p. 76; Wilcox, *Prefaces*, p. 116. The passage is understood differently by Mark Griffith, "How Much Latin Did Ælfric's *Magister* Know," *Notes and Queries*, 244 (1999), 177–81, according to whom competent instruction was available at the Old Minster in Winchester. Michael Lapidge suggests that this *magister* may have been Iorvert, a Welsh schoolmaster at Winchester: "Ælfric's Schooldays," in *Early Medieval English Texts and Interpretations: Presented to Donald G. Scragg*, ed. Elaine Treharne and Susan Rosser (Tempe, AZ, 2002), pp. 301–9, at 309.

Vivien Law deduced that Ælfric had been a student of Dunstan, the later archbishop of Canterbury; this study must therefore have taken place at Glastonbury sometime between 940 and 956. But the relevant sentence in the *Grammar*—"hwa lærde ðe?: Dunstan (taught me)"—is followed by the statement, "he ordained me" (He me hadode), where *he* refers equally to Dunstan (as an example of the use of a pronoun instead of a noun). But even if what is in question here is only the *ordinatio monachi* which Dunstan as abbot of Glastonbury, no later than 956 (or as bishop of London, 957×959–959), could have performed—the dating of Ælfric's birth on the basis of the first sentence becomes extremely problematic, because this date has hitherto been taken as ca. 950.[10] However, for his biography, education, and writings the decisive fact is one which he mentions and emphasizes on several occasions: that he was a student of Bishop Æthelwold in Winchester, and presumably more than a mere student in the circle of this esteemed teacher, and in that of Æthelwold's successor, Ælfheah. Æthelwold became bishop of Winchester in 963; he died in 984. Ælfric came to Winchester at the latest around 970 (where he was a witness to the consecration of Ælfstan as bishop of Ramsbury, which took place in 970), and in particular to the Old Minster there, which under Æthelwold had become a monastic cathedral (964) and at the same time the home of England's intellectual and religious elite.[11]

In about 987 Ælfric was sent as teacher to the newly founded abbey of Cerne in Dorset. Here—according to the traditional opinion—the majority of his writings were composed, and here he remained until 1005, when he was promoted to the abbacy of Eynsham in Oxfordshire. (From Eynsham derives the byname which is customarily used to identify our Ælfric.) But this picture is far from being secure in any respect. For one thing, Ælfric

10. Vivien Law, "Ælfric's *Excerptiones de arte grammatica anglice*," in *Grammar and Grammarians in the Early Middle Ages* (London, 1997), pp. 201–23, at 202 and n. 7 (first published 1987); she is followed by Wilcox in *Prefaces*, p. 7. Cf. however Godden, *Catholic Homilies* III. xxx. Mechthild Gretsch points out to me that the example cited by Law from the *Grammar* (8.13–15; cf. below, n. 21) most likely derives from the teaching of Æthelwold; the statements refer to Æthelwold's own life, and so do not reflect Ælfric's personal experience. On the *ordinatio monachi* in Anglo-Saxon England, see *The Claudius Pontificals*, ed. D. H. Turner, Henry Bradshaw Society 97 (1971), pp. xxxiii–xxxv, 97–103.

11. On Æthelwold and Winchester in the tenth century, see *Bishop Æthelwold: His Career and Influence*, ed. Barbara Yorke (Woodbridge, 1988); *Wulfstan of Winchester, Life of St. Æthelwold*, ed. Michael Lapidge and Michael Winterbottom (Oxford, 1991); Michael Lapidge, "Æthelwold," in *Blackwell Encyclopaedia*, p. 19; Mechthild Gretsch, *The Intellectual Foundations of the English Benedictine Reform*, CSASE 25 (Cambridge, 1999). On the date of Ælfric's entry into the Old Minster, see ch. 10 of his *Vita S. Æthelwoldi*, which is an abbreviated reworking of the earlier *Vita* by Wulfstan; cf. below, n. 24.

names Cerne Abbey as his residence on only one occasion, namely in the Old English preface to his First Series of *Catholic Homilies*, that is to say probably not later than 991. There is no evidence that Ælfric remained there for a longer period, and it is entirely possible that after some time he returned once more to Winchester. On the other hand, his writings imply not only wide reading but the use of a sizeable and accessible library. The new, small abbey in Dorset can scarcely have had such a library. Library visits to Winchester, and the loan of books from Winchester, could have provided some help, but there is no evidence whatsoever for these.[12]

It is incontestable, however, that in 1005 (or shortly before) Ælfric was called as abbot to Eynsham, like Cerne a newly founded abbey. This is clear from the preface of his "Letter" to the monks of Eynsham[13]—in fact a collection of instructions pertaining above all to the liturgy of Mass and Office— and it is astonishing that this preface (which is preserved together with the "Letter" in a single manuscript) did not receive scholarly attention until Dietrich. Only a few of Ælfric's writings can be dated to the period between 1005 and 1012 (at the latest), but nothing is known concerning the year of his death, nor about his immediate successors as abbots at Eynsham.[14]

12. But see Godden in *Catholic Homilies* III. xlv. On the history of the abbey of Cerne, see Wilcox, *Prefaces*, pp. 9–12, as well as *The Cerne Abbey Millennium Lectures*, ed. Katherine Barker (Cerne Abbas, 1988). The possibility that Ælfric could have been abbot of Cerne is not ruled out in *The Heads of Religious Houses: England and Wales. I: 940–1216*, ed. David Knowles et al., 2nd ed. (Cambridge, 2001), p. 37.

13. *Eynsham Letter*, ch. 1, p. 110; see also the extensive introduction by Christopher Jones.

14. Fundamental for the dating of Ælfric's writings is the pioneering article, first published in 1959, by Peter Clemoes, "The Chronology of Ælfric's Works," reprinted recently in *Old English Prose* (cited above, n. 1), pp. 29–72; supplementary information is provided by John Pope in *Homilies Suppl.*, I. 146–50. On the year of Ælfric's death, see Whitelock (cited below, n. 68).

ÆLFRIC'S WRITINGS AND THEIR CIRCULATION

What has been said hitherto concerning Ælfric's career suggests that he led the life of a monk, priest (as he designates himself from about 990), and abbot living in monastic seclusion. As we will see, his life seems to have been less secluded than one might expect. Before returning to this point, we may consider what it was that made him well known, indeed famous, namely his writings, of which we shall only treat the most important. All of these were produced during the period from ca. 987 to 1012. There are in general few doubts about the attribution of works to Ælfric, even in cases where he does not name himself as author.

Of writings in English pride of place belongs to more than 160 homilies (mostly exegetical in nature)[15] and saints' Lives;[16] it is above all from these writings that Ælfric derives his reputation as a master of Old English prose. To these are to be added translations and homiletic versions of parts of the

---

15. The homilies have all been edited in the great editions of Clemoes and Godden, *Catholic Homilies* I–III, of John Pope, *Homilies of Ælfric: A Supplementary Collection* (cf. the list of abbreviations above), and of Bruno Assmann, *Angelsächsische Homilien und Heiligenleben. Reprint with a Supplementary Introduction* by Peter Clemoes, Bibliothek der angelsächsischen Prosa III (Darmstadt, 1964; originally published 1889); a few further homilies are listed, with editions, by Angus Cameron, "A List of Old English Texts," in *A Plan for the Dictionary of Old English*, ed. Roberta Frank and Angus Cameron (Toronto, 1973), pp. 81–83. The introductions and notes to these editions by Clemoes, Godden, and Pope are fundamental. For over a century the *Catholic Homilies* were only available in the edition and translation (both remarkably competent, given the date) of Benjamin Thorpe: *The Homilies of the Anglo-Saxon Church. The First Part, Containing the Sermones Catholici, or Homilies of Ælfric*, 2 vols. (London, 1844–46). A few years after their publication, on 27 July 1850, Thorpe was elected, on the proposal of Johann Andreas Schmeller, as a Corresponding Fellow of the Bayerische Akademie der Wissenschaften: Richard J. Brunner, *Johann Andreas Schmeller und die Bayerische Akademie der Wissenschaften. Dokumente und Erläuterungen*, Bayer. Akad. der Wiss., Philosophisch-Historische Klasse, Abhandlungen N.F. 115 (Munich, 1997), pp. 470–76. The new edition of the *Catholic Homilies* by Clemoes and Godden was awarded the Sir Israel Gollancz Memorial Prize by the British Academy in October 2001: *The British Academy Review*, July–December 2001, p. 4. On the edition of *Catholic Homilies* I, see Donald Scragg, "Editing Ælfric's *Catholic Homilies*," *Anglia*, 121 (2003), 610–18. This is not the place to list references to the numerous studies, particularly of recent decades, on individual homilies and saints' Lives; see instead the bibliographies cited above, n. 1.

16. A number of Ælfric's saints' Lives are included in the *Catholic Homilies* I and II; a large collection of them, as contained in MS. Cotton Julius E. vii, is edited by Walter W. Skeat, *Ælfric's Lives of Saints*, EETS o.s. 76, 82, 94, 114 (1881–1900); four of the forty pieces in this manuscript (and edition) are not by Ælfric. The most important recent study of the Lives is by Mechthild Gretsch, *Ælfric and the Cult of Saints in Late Anglo-Saxon England*, CSASE 34 (Cambridge, 2005). See also Joyce Hill, "The Dissemination of Ælfric's *Lives of Saints*: A Preliminary

Old Testament, a summary of the entire Bible (the *Letter to Sigeweard*),[17] an abbreviated version of Alcuin's *Interrogationes Sigewulfi in Genesin*,[18] and a scientific handbook (*De temporibus anni*) on the creation, the sun, moon, stars and planets, the year and the seasons, the wind and the weather, derived principally from works by Bede.[19]

Ælfric's so-called "Pastoral Letters" were composed both in English and in Latin versions,[20] as also are the informative prefaces to his more important writings (*Catholic Homilies, Lives of Saints, Grammar*). Latin and Old English are combined—as necessitated by the subject matter—in his pioneering *Grammar* and the *Glossary*, a class glossary appended to the *Grammar*.[21]

Survey," in *Holy Men and Holy Women: Old English Prose Saints' Lives and Their Contexts*, ed. Paul E. Szarmach (Albany, NY, 1996), pp. 235–59; Michael Lapidge, "Ælfric's Sanctorale," ibid., pp. 115–29, as well as Wilcox, *Prefaces*, pp. 45–51. On the sources: Patrick H. Zettel, "Saints' Lives in Old English: Latin Manuscripts and Vernacular Accounts: Ælfric," *Peritia*, 1 (1982), 17–37. On manuscripts of Ælfric's Lives of Saints not collated by Skeat, see Aaron J Kleist, "Ælfric's Corpus: A Conspectus," *Florilegium*, 18 (2001), 113–64, at 154–55.

17. *The Old English Version of the Heptateuch, Ælfric's Treatise on the Old and New Testament and His Preface to Genesis*, ed. S. J. Crawford, EETS o.s. 160 (repr. 1969, with text of two additional manuscripts edited by N. R. Ker), to be replaced by *The Old English Heptateuch and Ælfric's "Libellus de ueteri testamento et nouo,"* vol. 1, ed. Richard Marsden, EETS o.s. 330 (2008). See also *The Old English Illustrated Hexateuch. British Museum Cotton Claudius B.IV*, ed. C. R. Dodwell and Peter A. M. Clemoes, EEMF 18 (Copenhagen, 1974), with an important introduction. Only a part of the Old English translation of the Pentateuch and Joshua is by Ælfric; see Pope, *Homilies Suppl.*, I. 143, where there is discussion (as also in Wilcox, *Prefaces*, pp. 42–43) of other Old Testament pieces by Ælfric. On the biblical text and the translation, see Richard Marsden, *The Text of the Old Testament in Anglo-Saxon England*, CSASE 15 (Cambridge, 1995), ch. 12, and idem, "Ælfric's Errors: The Evidence," *Essays for Joyce Hill on Her Sixtieth Birthday*, ed. Mary Swan, *Leeds Studies in English*, n.s. 37 (2006), 135–60. There are also several useful contributions in *The Old English Hexateuch: Aspects and Approaches*, ed. Rebecca Barnhouse and Benjamin C. Withers (Kalamazoo, MI: Medieval Institute Publications, 2000).

18. George E. MacLean, "Ælfric's Version of Alcuini Interrogationes Sigewulfi in Genesin," *Anglia*, 6 (1883), 425–73 and 7 (1884), 1–59; see also Angus Cameron, "A List of Old English Texts," p. 83. For a planned new edition cf. *Clavis Scriptorum Latinorum Medii Aevi: Auctores Galliae 735–987*, II, ed. Marie-Hélène Jullien and Françoise Perelman (Turnhout, 1999), pp. 485–88, where neither Ælfric nor the editions of MacLean and William Stoneman (Ph.D. diss., University of Toronto, 1982) are mentioned.

19. *Ælfric's De Temporibus Anni*, ed. Heinrich Henel, EETS o.s. 213 (1942); Malcolm Godden, in *An Eleventh-Century Anglo-Saxon Illustrated Miscellany. British Library Cotton Tiberius B. V Part I*, ed. Patrick McGurk et al., EEMF 21 (Copenhagen, 1983), pp. 59–64, on the origin and circulation of the work; there is also a useful survey in *Ælfwine's Prayerbook*, ed. Beate Günzel, Henry Bradshaw Society 108 (London,1993), pp. 35–44.

20. *Die Hirtenbriefe Ælfrics in altenglischer und lateinischer Fassung*, ed. Bernhard Fehr. *Reprint with a Supplement to the Introduction* by Peter Clemoes, Bibliothek der angelsächsischen Prosa IX (Darmstadt, 1966; first ed. 1914). Cf. below, n. 70.

21. *Ælfrics Grammatik und Glossar*, ed. Julius Zupitza; cf. below, n. 57, as well as Vivien Law, "Ælfric's *Excerptiones*" (above, n. 10).

Works composed entirely in Latin include a scholastic colloquy for educational purposes (known as the *Colloquium*),[22] his "Letter" to the monks of Eynsham,[23] and a Life of his master Æthelwold, which is an abbreviated version of the *Vita S. Æthelwoldi* by his fellow monk Wulfstan.[24] A few further treatises in Old English and some excerpts in Latin must be passed over here.[25]

This brief enumeration may have the effect of characterizing Ælfric principally as a translator and redactor, and he has occasionally been labeled as such by superficial observers; but such a characterization does not do justice to his achievement—and to his role in late Anglo-Saxon ecclesiastical and educational history. For one must not overlook the exceptional (but controlled) freedom which he exercised in the treatment of his sources, where he was following models; this alone, in combination with his stylistic mastery, enables his writings, particularly the homilies, to be classified not as translations but as re-creations. Nor should one overlook the scope and demands of the task which he set for himself in his work—or rather which were imposed on him by contemporary conditions and by his audience, which was in no sense only a narrow circle of monastic inmates but included ordinary lay persons as well as the nobility and the episcopacy.

In the Europe of Ælfric's time there is no author and no work in the vernacular which bears comparison with the impact and circulation of his writings. There exist today twenty-four manuscripts which preserve his *Catholic Homilies* complete or in large part, to which may be added nine fragments of similar manuscripts, and a further six which preserve at least one or two of his homilies. Of his *De temporibus* eight manuscripts and fragments have been preserved, and of his *Grammar*, twelve more or less complete manu-

22. *Ælfric's Colloquy,* ed. G. N. Garmonsway, rev. ed. (Exeter, 1978, first publ. 1939); for the extensive secondary literature, see below, n. 61.

23. *Eynsham Letter.* Jones's edition supersedes all previous editions.

24. Preserved in a single manuscript (Paris, BNF, lat. 5362, ca. 1100, English?) and edited most recently as Appendix A in *Vita Æthelwoldi,* pp. 70–80; there is an English translation in *English Historical Documents* I, *c. 500–1042,* ed. Dorothy Whitelock, 2nd ed. (London, 1979), pp. 903–11.

25. A complete list of all the Old English texts is found in Cameron, "A List of Old English Texts," pp. 44–88, in Pope, "The Ælfric Canon," in *Homilies Suppl.,* I. 136–45, and in Kleist, "Ælfric's Corpus: A Conspectus" (cited above, n. 16). On the Latin texts and excerpts, see Christopher A. Jones, "*Meatim sed et Rustica:* Ælfric of Eynsham as a Medieval Latin Author," *Journal of Medieval Latin,* 8 (1998), 1–57.

scripts, together with two fragments and later transcriptions of manuscripts which have subsequently been lost.[26]

On the face of it, these may not seem like very impressive numbers. But one must bear in mind that manuscripts containing texts in Old English had a very low survival rate after the twelfth century, when, because of rapid changes in the English language, there was scarcely anyone who could read and understand them.[27] Furthermore, the dissolution of the monasteries by Henry VIII, during the years 1536–39, had disastrous consequences for the preservation of manuscripts, for it was precisely in the Benedictine foundations and refoundations of the tenth and eleventh centuries that manuscripts of the Anglo-Saxon period were preserved in monastic libraries, whose holdings were in many cases carelessly dispersed and lost.[28] Of the thousands of manuscripts which were produced in England between the late seventh century and the end of the eleventh or were imported into England from overseas, we have today only about twelve hundred (not counting single-sheet charters), often preserved only as fragments. Among these there are more than sixty containing writings of Ælfric.[29] The Leipzig Anglo-Saxonist Richard Wülker long ago conjectured that the Danes (above all during the plundering and warfare of the ninth century) and Normans destroyed less than one-tenth of what, during the sixteenth century, when the monasteries were suppressed, the English themselves destroyed; for the Anglo-Saxon manuscripts, this conjecture may not be far from the truth.[30]

26. See Milton McC. Gatch, "The Achievement of Ælfric and His Colleagues in European Perspective," in *The Old English Homily and Its Backgrounds*, ed. Paul E. Szarmach and Bernard F. Huppé (Albany, NY, 1978), pp. 43–73; on the manuscript transmission of Ælfric's writings, see Ker, *Catalogue*, pp. 511–18.

27. On knowledge of Old English in the Middle English period, see Ker, *Catalogue*, p. xlix; Hans Sauer, "Knowledge of Old English in the Middle English Period?" in *Language History and Linguistic Modelling: A Festschrift for Jacek Fisiak on His 60th Birthday*, ed. Raymond Hickey and Stanislaw Puppel (Berlin, 1997), pp. 791–814; Timothy Graham, "The Beginnings of Old English Studies: Evidence from the Manuscripts of Matthew Parker," in *Back to the Manuscripts*, ed. Shugi Sato (Tokyo, 1997), pp. 29–50, esp. p. 29, and the literature there cited; Franzen, *Tremulous Hand* (cited above, n. 4).

28. On the historical background, see Dom David Knowles, *The Religious Orders in England*, vol. 3: *The Tudor Age* (Cambridge, 1959); on the libraries, see C. E. Wright, "The Dispersal of the Libraries in the Sixteenth Century," in *The English Library before 1700: Studies in Its History*, ed. Francis Wormald and C. E. Wright (London, 1958), pp. 148–75; Helmut Gneuss, "Englands Bibliotheken im Mittelalter und ihr Untergang," in *Books and Libraries in Early England* (Aldershot, 1996), no. I, esp. pp. 112–21 (first published 1964). On the early efforts to save manuscripts from destruction, see Keynes, *Bibliography*, pp. 262–68.

29. All manuscripts and fragments, as presently known, are listed in Gneuss, *Handlist* (cited above, n. 2); see also Lapidge, *Library*.

30. Richard Wülker, *Grundriss zur Geschichte der angelsächsischen Litteratur* (Leipzig, 1885), p. 4.

This is not an appropriate place to treat this chapter of English library history. A question which arises, however, concerns the astonishing success and survival rate of Ælfric's principal writings—the *Catholic Homilies, De temporibus anni, Grammar and Glossary*, and probably the *Lives of Saints*. They were all produced before the period of Ælfric's abbacy at Eynsham. What can account for the wide circulation of these works, if their author was at first an entirely unknown monk, and—if we assume that he remained at Cerne—one who was domiciled in a small and remote minster in southwest England? In several of these writings one finds references to the commissioning or the requests of the aristocracy of Wessex (*Lives of Saints*, translation of Genesis), or at least to their interest;[31] in others, however—as in the case of the widely used *Grammar*—there is no such reference, and one must suppose that in these cases Ælfheah, bishop of Winchester (984–1006), and Sigeric, archbishop of Canterbury (990–94; Ælfric sent exemplars to him of both series of *Catholic Homilies*), were instrumental in the circulation of these writings, if indeed they had not commissioned them. In this connection the conjecture first expressed by Dietrich, that Ælfric, after some time spent at Cerne, returned to the Old Minster in Winchester, would find substantiation and corroboration.[32]

---

31. See Ælfric's prefaces, and discussion below, p. 29, and nn. 72 and 73.
32. Dietrich, "Abt Aelfrik," *Zeitschrift für die historische Theologie*, 26 (1856), 244–45.

ÆLFRIC'S HOMILETIC WRITINGS

Literary history of the Anglo-Saxon period long focused its attention on Old English poetry, and, especially in the beginning, on the search to identify pagan elements.[33] Meanwhile, it is incontestable that Old English literature had its roots in the Christian-Latin tradition, and the prose came increasingly to receive the attention it deserves. The homiletic writings of Ælfric played a principal role in this revaluation, given that complete copies (or excerpts), particularly of the *Catholic Homilies*, were to be found circulating throughout the entire country, up into the twelfth century.

The impetus for the production of these homilies came from necessity. In England there was no doubt about the duty of priests to preach regularly, on each Sunday and feastday, or at least every fortnight, as specified in the *Rule for Canons* by Bishop Chrodegang (enlarged version, chap. 42), a work which probably was translated into English at the Old Minster in Winchester during Ælfric's time there. That the preaching should be *on englisc* (or: *propria lingua*) is specified expressly by Ælfric in his Pastoral Letters;[34] but the fact that this did not take place, or only rarely, provided the motive for Ælfric's composition of his homily collections—whether in response to instructions or encouragement from higher ecclesiastical authority must remain an open question. That it was a monk who provided a preaching manual for the use of secular priests is not in itself unusual at that time; it is widely recognized nowadays that the Anglo-Saxon monasteries of the Benedictine reform movement participated actively in the pastoral care of the areas in which they were located; it is certain in any case that divine services in monastic churches were also attended by members of the lay public.[35] It

33. See now the important study by Eric Gerald Stanley, *Imagining the Anglo-Saxon Past: The Search for Anglo-Saxon Paganism, and Anglo-Saxon Trial by Jury* (Cambridge, 2000; earlier versions of the first part date from 1964–65 and 1975). On the subsequent shift in emphasis in the writing of Anglo-Saxon literary history, see Stanley B. Greenfield and Daniel G. Calder, *A New Critical History of Old English Literature: With a Survey of the Anglo-Latin Background* by Michael Lapidge (New York, 1986).

34. *Hirtenbriefe*, I. 61, 2.159; cf. *Wulfstan's Canon Law Collection*, ed. J. E. Cross and Andrew Hamer (Cambridge, 1999), p. 115, B. 4, and *Wulfstan's Canons of Edgar*, ed. Roger Fowler, EETS o.s. 266 (1972), ch. 52.

35. See Mary Clayton, "Homiliaries and Preaching in Anglo-Saxon England," in *Old English Prose* (cited above, n. 1), pp. 151–98, esp. 179–86 (first published 1985); Milton McC. Gatch, *Preaching and Theology in Anglo-Saxon England: Ælfric and Wulfstan* (Toronto, 1977); John

is entirely conceivable that Ælfric preached his own homilies in Cerne (or Winchester).

Ælfric saw as his task the composition of a corpus of homilies that could be used throughout the church year. The extremely complex story of the production of this corpus, which has only been unraveled in recent times, can only be mentioned briefly here.[36] Ælfric first composed (in roughly 990) a cycle of forty homilies, designated as *Sermones Catholici* in the manuscripts (the First Series of *Catholic Homilies*), in which he was concerned above all with explanation of the gospel pericopes for the most important feastdays and Sundays of the liturgical year. A few years later followed a second cycle, once again with forty items, which were intended to fill gaps in the original series (particularly for the Sundays after Epiphany and Whitsun), and to provide a multipurpose *Commune Sanctorum* and, in addition to feasts of the apostles (included in the First and Second Series), also homilies for saints who were particularly venerated in England (Gregory the Great, Benedict, Cuthbert, and also Martin).[37] As Ælfric suggested, the second cycle could either be used for a second year, or could be combined with the first cycle (as in the manuscripts Bodley 340 and 342) in such a way that the pericopes of most Sundays and feastdays of a year would be supplied with exegetical homilies.[38] About half of the homilies required for the Sundays after Easter and Whitsun were, however, still lacking. In later years Ælfric enlarged the program by adding further homilies. Furthermore, he selected for translation a sizeable number of saints' Lives from the monastic legendary (*Lives of Saints*); these, however, may not have been intended for preaching to the laity.

The importance of Ælfric's corpus of homilies becomes clear as soon as one reflects that Ælfric produced preaching texts, in the people's own

---

Blair, "Parochial Organization," in *Blackwell Encyclopaedia*, pp. 356–58; idem, *The Church in Anglo-Saxon Society* (Oxford, 2005), and see the contributions to *Pastoral Care in Late Anglo-Saxon England*, ed. Francesca Tinti (Woodbridge, 2005). The reference to *fidelem plebem* (glossed *geleafful folc* in MS. Cotton Tiberius A. iii) attending mass in a monastic church, in ch. 23 of the *Regularis Concordia* (see below, n. 75), is an important testimony.

36. Treated briefly by Clemoes, "Chronology" (cited above, n. 14), and exhaustively in *Catholic Homilies* I. 65–168; see also Godden in *Catholic Homilies* II. lxxviii–xciv.

37. For these, see Gretsch, *Ælfric and the Cult of Saints* (cited above, n. 16).

38. *Catholic Homilies* I. 173–74. On the system of pericopes, which provide the basis of Ælfric's homilies (including those which have been transmitted independently of the *Catholic Homilies*), see the definitive study by Ursula Lenker, *Die westsächsische Evangelienversion und die Perikopenordnungen im angelsächsischen England*, TUEPh 20 (Munich, 1997), pp. 498–500 and passim.

language, that could be used throughout England, for the entire liturgical year, an achievement which until then had had no parallel either in England or on the European continent. With his translations of the pericopes Ælfric had also made available in English substantial portions of the Gospels. Apparently, he chose to supplant (the use of) the text of the so-called West Saxon Gospels, which date from the tenth century, and which Ælfric certainly knew.[39] Finally, the complete corpus of his homilies supplied at the same time an all-encompassing and reliable compendium of the Christian religion.[40] Nor should it be forgotten that there were Old English homilies, likewise intended to explain gospel pericopes, in existence before Ælfric; two such collections of texts are preserved in the *Blickling Homilies* and the *Vercelli Homilies*. But as far as the cycle of the church year is concerned, what they offer is merely fragmentary; furthermore, these earlier homilies made use of sources the content of which Ælfric regarded as *gedwyld*, that is to say, untrustworthy, misleading, and even heretical, by which he meant apocryphal writings such as the *Visio Pauli*, and against which he maintained a strictly orthodox position in all his writings.[41]

It was in the nature of the enterprise that Ælfric's homilies could not be original compositions. A rich supply of exegetical homilies, which had been composed in the patristic period and later, was already to hand. Ælfric stated his relationship to this tradition in the Latin preface to his First Series of *Catholic Homilies*: "Hos namque auctores in hac explanatione

---

39. *The Old English Version of the Gospels*, ed. R. M. Liuzza. I: *Text and Introduction*; II: *Notes and Glossary*, EETS o.s. 304, 314 (1994–2000); on the translators, see II. 100–119, as well as Lenker, *Evangelienversion*, pp. 47–54.

40. See in particular Lynne Grundy, *Books and Grace: Ælfric's Theology*, King's College London Medieval Studies VI (London, 1991), and the literature there cited; Peter Clemoes, "Ælfric," in *Continuations and Beginnings: Studies in Old English Literature*, ed. Eric Gerald Stanley (London, 1966), pp. 176–209, as well as various studies by Malcolm Godden (listed *Catholic Homilies* III. xiv).

41. On the earlier homily tradition, see D. G. Scragg, "The Corpus of Vernacular Homilies and Prose Saints' Lives before Ælfric," *ASE*, 8 (1979), 223–77. On Ælfric's strict rejection of everything which he saw as unorthodox and apocryphal, see Clemoes, "Ælfric" (cited above, n. 40), pp. 184, 189, and especially Mary Clayton, *The Cult of the Virgin Mary in Anglo-Saxon England*, CSASE 2 (Cambridge, 1990), pp. 260–66 and passim, as well as Clayton, *The Apocryphal Gospels of Mary in Anglo-Saxon England*, CSASE 26 (Cambridge, 1998), pp. 110–11; see also Wilcox, *Prefaces*, pp. 27–31, and now the articles by Frederick M. Biggs and Thomas N. Hall in *Apocryphal Texts and Traditions in Anglo-Saxon England*, ed. Kathryn Powell and Donald Scragg (Cambridge, 2003). Ælfric must certainly have known the *Decretum (Pseudo-)Gelasianum de libris recipiendis et non recipiendis*, given that a copy of this work is included in a collection of texts assembled by him, namely that in Boulogne-sur-Mer 63, fols. 1–34, on which see esp. Lapidge, *Vita Æthelwoldi*, pp. cxlvii–cxlviii, and Joyce Hill, "Ælfric, Gelasius, and St. George," *Mediaevalia*, 11 (1989), 1–17.

sumus secuti, videlicet Augustinum Ypponiensem, Hieronimum, Bedam, Gregorium, Smaragdum et aliquando Hægmonem, horum denique auctoritas ab omnibus catholicis libentissime suscipitur."[42] Research into Ælfric's sources had at first concentrated on these authors (or compilers, as in the case of Smaragdus and Haimo of Auxerre), as in the pioneering research of Max Förster dating from 1892–94. In the intervening years, however, it has become clear that Ælfric did not or not always consult the homilies of the church fathers and Bede directly in manuscripts of their writings but rather through the medium of a work in which a comprehensive selection of such homilies had already been assembled, namely the Homiliary of Paul the Deacon, which was compiled in the 790s at the instigation of Charlemagne.[43] The materials Ælfric drew on in his homilies were of course originally intended as readings for the Night Office, and they were adopted as such during the Benedictine reform movement in England, if not earlier.[44] But Paul the Deacon's Homiliary also provided an excellent foundation for the composition of sermons addressed to a lay public and preached perhaps within the framework of the Mass. Unfortunately we do not know, or know with certainty, the precise form of the exemplar of Paul's Homiliary which Ælfric had before him. The original Homiliary of Paul was subsequently amplified through the incorporation of large numbers of additional homilies; this process of amplification remains to be properly elucidated. In any case the Homiliary in its expanded form was brought to England during the course of the tenth century.

42. On Ælfric's sources for his homilies, see Pope, *Homilies Suppl.*, I. 150–77, Godden in *Catholic Homilies* III. xxxviii–lxii and passim, as well as Wilcox, *Prefaces*, pp. 23–30. A detailed inventory of sources is available on the database of the research project *Fontes Anglo-Saxonici*, accessible at <http://fontes.english.ox.ac.uk/>, and now in Lapidge, *Library*, pp. 350–66.

43. Cyril L. Smetana, "Paul the Deacon's Patristic Anthology," in *The Old English Homily and Its Backgrounds* (cited above, n. 26), pp. 75–97; Smetana, "Ælfric and the Early Medieval Homiliary," *Traditio*, 15 (1959), 163–204; Lenker, *Evangelienversion*, p. 493; Joyce Hill, "Translating the Tradition: Manuscripts, Models and Methodologies in the Composition of Ælfric's *Catholic Homilies*," The Toller Memorial Lecture 1996, *Bulletin of the John Rylands University Library of Manchester*, 79 (1997), 43–65, where she explains (p. 52) the striking fact that Ælfric nowhere names the Homiliary of Paul the Deacon as a source.—Mary Clayton, "Homiliaries and Preaching" (cited above, n. 35) is fundamental. The useful works of Max Förster on Ælfric are listed by Reinsma; see p. 285. Förster had already mentioned the Homiliary of Paul the Deacon as a possible source of Ælfric: "Über die Quellen von Ælfric's exegetischen Homiliae Catholicae," *Anglia*, 16 (1894), 1–61, at pp. 58–59 with n. 1.

44. Robert Stanton, *The Culture of Translation in Anglo-Saxon England* (Cambridge, 2002), p. 162, claims about the *Catholic Homilies* that "monks used them in their daily office." But it should be remembered that there is no evidence whatsoever that any parts of Mass or Office were read or sung in the vernacular in Anglo-Saxon England; see David N. Dumville, *Liturgy and the Ecclesiastical History of Late Anglo-Saxon England* (Woodbridge, 1992), pp. 127–32, on the strictly limited role of Old English in liturgical books.

In order to appreciate Ælfric's own achievement and his pedagogic and pastoral intentions, it is essential to recognize that what he accomplished was in no sense merely the translation of the wording of a Latin homily. In his homilies he also drew on a number of well-known authors and writings which he did not name in his preface, and which are not included in Paul the Deacon's Homiliary, such as (for example) various writings by Bede: the *Historia ecclesiastica gentis Anglorum*, the Commentaries on Mark and Luke, the *Vitae* of St. Cuthbert.

Finally, the ways and means by which Ælfric dealt with his sources is extremely important. He always kept in mind his public and his fundamental goal—the *edificatio simplicium*, the 'instruction of simple folk'. Hence the selection and combination of sources, expansions, abbreviations, transpositions, simplifications, brief historical and geographical explanations where necessary, biblical etymologies, and vivid allegorical and typological exposition, all contributed to this end, as did Ælfric's clear prose and unmatched preaching style.[45]

---

45. On Ælfric's working methods and technique of translation, see Clemoes, "Ælfric"; Godden in *Catholic Homilies* III. xlv and particularly the exemplary commentary in this volume, as well as Lapidge in *Vita Æthelwoldi*, pp. cxlvii–cxlix, Jones, "*Meatim sed et Rustica*" (cited above, n. 25), and Wilcox, *Prefaces*, pp. 53 and 63–65. That Ælfric in his later homilies no longer had in mind a lay public is suggested by Mary Clayton, "Homiliaries and Preaching in Anglo-Saxon England" (cited above, n. 35), pp. 186–87.

Ælfric's Language and Style

Ælfric is seen by students of English philology not as a theologian but above all as a master of vernacular prose style. But his role in the history of the English language extends further still; his stylistic intentions were bound up with an all-encompassing linguistic skill and command, in Latin as well as English, and a linguistic awareness which no previous English author had possessed, and which cannot be paralleled until long after Ælfric's death.[46]

When Ælfric repeatedly exhorts future copyists of his writings to work carefully, he naturally has in mind the contents of the writings. But he was also very concerned with the preservation of their linguistic form, on which he himself placed great value, as may be seen from his revision of the *Catholic Homilies*.[47] What is in question here is Standard Old English, the written form of the vernacular which, from the late tenth century onwards, was used throughout England. Standard Old English is characterized by consistent orthography and inflectional forms, whose origin is to be sought in the dialect of southwest England, but its enduring success and survival was prevented as a result of the Norman Conquest.[48]

46. See Malcolm Godden, "Literary Language," in *The Cambridge History of the English Language*, I. 490–535, and Janet Bately, "The Nature of Old English Prose," in *The Cambridge Companion to Old English Literature*, ed. Malcolm Godden and Michael Lapidge (Cambridge, 1991), pp. 71–87. On Ælfric's language (phonology, morphology, syntax), see Pope, *Homilies Suppl.*, I. 177–85, and Kleist, "Annotated Bibliography" (cited above, n. 1), nos. 57–78. On Ælfric's style, see also Clemoes, "Ælfric," and below, nn. 52–54.

47. Particularly instructive is Ælfric's warning to the copyists of his *Grammar*, p. 3. For other examples of such warnings, and for the eventuality of what he feared most, see Mary Swan, "Memorialized Readings: Manuscript Evidence for Old English Homily Composition," in *Anglo-Saxon Manuscripts and Their Heritage*, ed. Phillip Pulsiano and Elaine M. Treharne (Aldershot, 1998), pp. 206–17. See also Malcolm Godden, "Old English Composite Homilies from Winchester," *ASE*, 4 (1975), 57–65, on the use of excerpts from Ælfric's writings; on manuscripts in which the homilies of Ælfric are combined with anonymous pieces, see Scragg, "The Corpus of Vernacular Homilies and Prose Saints' Lives before Ælfric" (cited above, n. 41)—combined, that is, against Ælfric's express wishes: *Catholic Homilies* II, "Explicit," p. 345, lines 7–9.

48. See most recently and most clearly Mechthild Gretsch, "Winchester Vocabulary and Standard Old English: The Vernacular in Late Anglo-Saxon England," The Toller Memorial Lecture 2000, *Bulletin of the John Rylands University Library of Manchester*, 83 (2002 for 2001), 3–49, as well as Gretsch, "In Search of Standard Old English," in *Bookmarks from the Past: Studies in Early English Language and Literature in Honour of Helmut Gneuss*, ed. Lucia Kornexl and Ursula Lenker, TUEPh 30 (Frankfurt a.M., 2003), pp. 33–67, and eadem, "A Key to Ælfric's Standard Old English," *Essays for Joyce Hill* (cited above, n. 17), pp. 161–77. Cf. below, n. 51.

That what is in question is a regularized form of language is clear from the fact that more recent developments, particularly in the inflectional system, are not reflected in the conservative practices of scribes. The desired consistency is attested very early on, in the earliest manuscript of the *Catholic Homilies* (First Series; B.L. Royal 7. C. xii), the preparation and writing of which was undoubtedly overseen by Ælfric himself. Here are preserved more than 19,000 forms, from a total of 1,511 Old English substantives (leaving aside foreign loanwords and personal names), whose inflectional endings, for case and number, show virtually no departures from their respective declensional models.[49]

However, Ælfric aspired not only to consistency in matters of inflectional forms but also to consistency and regularity in syntax, word formation, and word usage. In the case of syntax, this may be seen above all in alterations made to the aforementioned Royal manuscript and from comparison with later copies of the homily texts. Ælfric regularized his use of noun cases with prepositions—here the model of Latin grammar probably played a role—and he clearly concerned himself with the designation of the future tense through choice of particular forms of the *verbum substantivum*.[50] In his word usage the West Saxon basis of Standard Old English undoubtedly played a role, as probably also did Ælfric's place of birth (even though we do not know precisely where this was). Noteworthy in particular is his systematic choice of words in particular semantic fields. This choice can be convincingly attributed to his Winchester schooling; indeed, it is not out of the question that, as a member of the scholarly circle of his master Æthelwold, he himself was involved in this process of lexical selection.[51]

Ælfric writes clear, unmannered, and easily comprehensible prose. This is true above all for his Old English writings, but it is also true of those written in Latin. In this respect he stands apart from the English prose written before him, which naturally stood in need of development and

49. As demonstrated in Connie Clare Eble, "Noun Inflection in Royal 7 C.XII, Ælfric's First Series of Catholic Homilies," Ph.D. diss., University of North Carolina at Chapel Hill, 1970 (unpublished).

50. On this see Kenneth Sisam, *Studies in the History of Old English Literature* (Oxford, 1953), pp. 179–85; Clemoes in *Ælfric's First Series of Catholic Homilies, British Museum Royal 7 C.XII, Fols. 4-218*, ed. Norman Eliason and Peter Clemoes, EEMF 13 (Copenhagen, 1966), pp. 32–33, and in *Catholic Homilies* I. 128; Godden in *The Cambridge History of the English Language* I. 519, and idem, "Ælfric as Grammarian: The Evidence of his *Catholic Homilies*," in *Early Medieval English Texts and Interpretations* (cited above, n. 9), pp. 13–29.

51. Walter Hofstetter, *Winchester und der spätaltenglische Sprachgebrauch. Untersuchungen zur geographischen und zeitlichen Verbreitung altenglischer Synonyme*, TUEPh 14 (Munich, 1987); Gretsch, *The Intellectual Foundations of the English Benedictine Reform* (cited above, n. 11).

improvement (I say this without intending to belittle the achievement of King Alfred and his circle). He also stands apart from the "hermeneutic" Latin which was practiced widely in England by his contemporaries, and was even promoted and practiced by his teacher Æthelwold, and which is particularly characterized by learned-sounding vocabulary: archaisms, neologisms, and graecisms. Ælfric, however, makes his attitude to this style unambiguously clear in his prefaces: he will not employ *obscura verba*, nor *garrula verbositas*, but will reproduce his sources *simplici et aperta locutione*.[52]

Ælfric himself specifies the reasons for this decision: he does not wish to be praised for *artificiosi sermonis compositio*; he writes his homilies and saints' Lives for listeners (and readers: *sive legendo sive audiendo*) including those who are uneducated. But I have no doubt that it was Ælfric's linguistic control and sense of style that decided the issue. He saw what could be achieved in Latin composition, and what the English language had to achieve by different means; accordingly, by choosing a spare but precise style, without *obscura verba* (of which there were plenty in currency in the English of his time),[53] and, by means of prudent curtailment of his sentence construction, he accomplished at one stroke his educational aims and his stylistic ideals.

At the same time it should not be forgotten that Ælfric's training and education also involved some study of classical rhetoric, naturally within the means by which it was accessible in late Anglo-Saxon England. Modern attempts to explain the structure of Ælfric's homilies in terms of ancient rhetorical discourse must, however, be seen as anachronistic. Ælfric in fact did make use of rhetorical devices, but in moderation. "Klarheit und Kürze, einfacher statt ausgeschmückter Stil, *abbreviatio* versus *amplificatio*, ist generell Ælfrics Prinzip für seine Predigten."[54]

In one respect, however, Ælfric set himself apart by using a stylistic device which came to characterize his writings from the time he first introduced it into some homilies in the Second Series of the *Catholic Homilies*. It consists in the rhythmic patterning of his prose, in which two consecutive

---

52. Michael Lapidge, "The Hermeneutic Style in Anglo-Latin Literature," *ASE*, 4 (1975), 67–111, reprinted with extensive addenda in Lapidge, *Anglo-Latin Literature 900–1066* (London, 1993), pp. 103–49 and 474–79. On Ælfric's Latin style, see Jones in *Eynsham Letter*, pp. 51–58, and in "*Meatim sed et Rustica*" (cited above, n. 25). Cf. Ælfric's comments (quoted above) on his Old English style in the prefaces to his *Catholic Homilies* I and II as well as the *Lives of Saints*.

53. See Gretsch, *The Intellectual Foundations of the English Benedictine Reform*, ch. 3.

54. "Clarity and concision, the simple in lieu of the ornate, *abbreviatio* in lieu of *amplificatio*, are the general principles which Ælfric followed in his homilies." Thus Gabriele Knappe, *Traditionen der klassischen Rhetorik im angelsächsischen England*, Anglistische Forschungen 236

syntactical units, or phrases, each having two principal accents, are linked to each other by means of alliteration; several pairs of units linked in this way go to make up the superior syntactic unit, the sentence. In this connection one thinks naturally of the form of Old English (and Germanic) alliterative verse; yet Ælfric's rhythmic prose remains clearly distinct from the verse. It lacks poetic vocabulary, in particular the numerous poetic compounds coined by poets; above all, it lacks the syntactic and stylistic peculiarities of poetry, for example, variation. Moreover, in spite of certain rhythmical liberties, verse composition follows the strict rules which were first elucidated by Eduard Sievers. Ælfric did not consider himself subject to these rules; in matters of syllable-count and number and positioning of accent, not to mention alliteration, he frequently departs from them. In a word, they were not rules for him; he freely adapted the basic structure of verse to serve as the framework for his rhythmical prose. That vernacular verse provided the stimulus for his prose is now regarded as certain. Latin models have also been proposed, with attention focused particularly on rhythmical clausulae, but without conviction; for even if thorough training and wide reading in Latin are well attested for Ælfric, his prose is so similar to Old English verse that a crucial link between the two cannot be denied.[55]

Another question, however, is why Ælfric, who in the First Series of *Catholic Homilies* had preferred a simple prose style, should subsequently have opted for the rhythmic style. The answer here lies without doubt in the destination which he sought for his writings, above all for the homilies and saints' Lives. They were specifically intended to be read aloud, for public presentation before a public which even at the turn of the first millennium was still thoroughly familiar with the Anglo-Saxon tradition of (oral) poetic composition; the older poetry was still being copied and transmitted, and new poetry, even poetry treating contemporary subjects, was being composed in the traditional style and verse-form, as for example the poem on

---

(Heidelberg, 1996), p. 392, in what is now the standard treatment of this subject, containing extensive reference to the writings of Ælfric. See also Mark Griffith, "Ælfric's Preface to Genesis: Genre, Rhetoric and the Origins of the *Ars dictaminis*," *ASE*, 29 (2000), 215–34.

55. The most thorough and illuminating treatment of "Ælfric's Rhythmical Prose" is to be found in Pope, *Homilies Suppl.*, I. 105–36. Cf. also Clemoes in *Catholic Homilies* I. xxxvi–xxxvii, and Knappe, *Traditionen der klassischen Rhetorik*, pp. 389–91, as well as Paul E. Szarmach, "Abbot Ælfric's Rhythmical Prose and the Computer Age," in *New Approaches to Editing Old English Verse*, ed. Sarah Larratt Keefer and Katherine O'Brien O'Keeffe (Cambridge, 1998), pp. 95–108. More recently, however, Thomas A. Bredehoft has strongly argued that Ælfric's compositions in what used to be called "rhythmical prose" are better identified as verse: "Ælfric and Late Old English Verse," *ASE*, 33 (2004), 77–107.

the battle of Maldon, concerning a historical event securely datable to 991, which was undoubtedly composed in Ælfric's lifetime.[56] So it is scarcely surprising that Ælfric realized the possibility of achieving greater effectiveness and more enthusiastic reception for his writings by use of this newly created rhythmical style.

56. See most recently *The Battle of Maldon AD 991*, ed. Donald Scragg (Oxford, 1991), and *The Battle of Maldon: Fiction and Fact*, ed. Janet Cooper (London, 1993).

Ælfric as Language Teacher

Ælfric's masterly skill as a teacher and scholar is fully revealed in his *Grammar*. Although for a long time its place in literary history was regarded as marginal by students of English philology, its pioneering importance in the history of linguistics and language teaching has now been recognized and appreciated. It would be appropriate to devote an entire lecture to the *Grammar* alone; I limit myself here to a few substantial points.[57]

Ælfric's *Grammar* is the earliest Latin grammar written in English, and moreover the first in any vernacular language. Whether it was produced in response to official encouragement—say, from Bishop Ælfheah, who certainly knew Ælfric's capabilities and must have prized them greatly—is not clear from the two prefaces of the *Grammar*. But the work's swift and wide circulation implies at least the support of higher authorities. It was produced soon after 992, probably in Cerne, and by the early eleventh century copies must have been found in every monastery and library in England. As we read in the Latin preface, the book was directed principally at monastic schools and their *pueruli*, that is to say oblates, but it must surely also have been of service in the education of older *conversi*.[58]

Ælfric's chosen task was obviously pressing, but not simple: it was necessary for him to impart a sound knowledge of a completely foreign language. To judge from the surviving manuscripts, few texts of Latin grammars were available in late Anglo-Saxon England; these and others, which could have been imported from the Continent, were scarcely suitable for the task. With few exceptions, these (late antique) Latin grammars had been composed

---

57. The standard edition of the *Grammar* is, and remains, that of Julius Zupitza, *Ælfrics Grammatik und Glossar* (first published Berlin, 1880), most recently reprinted Hildesheim 2001, with a new introduction and bibliography by Helmut Gneuss; see also Gneuss, "Ælfrics Grammatik und *Glossar*: Sprachwissenschaft um die Jahrtausendwende in England," in *Heilige und profane Sprachen*, ed. Werner Hüllen and Friederike Klippel (Wolfenbüttel, 2002), pp. 77–92, as well as n. 59.

58. On monastic schools from the period of the English Benedictine reform movement (in which pupils were also taught who were not meant to become monks or priests), as well as on *oblati* and *conversi*, see Dom David Knowles, *The Monastic Order in England*, 2nd ed. (Cambridge, 1963), pp. 487–89 and ch. XXIV, and now Mayke de Jong, *In Samuel's Image: Child Oblation in the Early Medieval West* (Leiden, 1996), especially on the earlier Anglo-Saxon period; Christopher A. Jones, "The Irregular Life in Ælfric Bata's Colloquies," in *Essays for Joyce Hill* (cited above, n. 17), pp. 241–60.

for native speakers of Latin and were therefore inappropriate for Ælfric's purposes: that is to say, they were either insufficiently comprehensive (apart from pedagogical shortcomings) or else were too ambitious and too loaded with detail, such as the *Institutiones grammaticae* of Priscian. On the other hand, what Ælfric had in mind, and what he then produced, was a thorough treatment especially of Latin inflectional morphology (a subject which presented great difficulties for English students). Systematic treatment of phonology and orthography, as well as of syntax (which was partially covered by the treatment of the parts of speech), needed less attention.

It was therefore essential for Ælfric either to find a suitable model or to write a new grammar. We now know the model which he chose: the treatise preserved in three manuscripts and entitled *Excerptiones de Prisciano*, which essentially consisted of Latin excerpts—as the name implies—from the *Institutiones* of Priscian. It is not entirely out of the question that these excerpts were compiled by Ælfric himself (this is a problem which could not be easily addressed as long as the *Excerptiones* remained unpublished). Ælfric's achievement consists in the abbreviation (for pedagogical purposes) and reworking of the *Excerptiones*, and above all in the addition of English translations not only of the definitions and explanations but also of all the words and sentences cited by way of example. In this way he produced a work which could also help those unfamiliar with Latin to "teach themselves" (as we would now say).[59]

Ælfric's goal, however, was more ambitious than that: in both of his prefaces he notes that his *Grammar* could help towards the understanding of *both* languages (*utramque linguam*). This remark should not be misunderstood: Ælfric naturally did not, and could not, wish to offer a systematic grammar of Old English. Rather, he saw that he had provided in his Latin grammar a useful model, too, for the description of the English of his own

---

59. The problem of Latin language teaching in early England is addressed by Vivien Law, "The Study of Latin Grammar in Eighth-Century Southumbria," in *Grammar and Grammarians in the Early Middle Ages* (Harlow, 1997), pp. 91–123, first published in 1983; on the Late Latin grammarians and their transmission in Anglo-Saxon England, see Vivien Law, *The Insular Latin Grammarians* (Woodbridge, 1982), and Helmut Gneuss, "The Study of Language in Anglo-Saxon England," in *Language and History in Early England* (Aldershot, 1996), no. III, first published in 1990. On Ælfric's model see Vivien Law, "Ælfric's *Excerptiones*" (cited above, n. 10). An edition has recently appeared: *Excerptiones de Prisciano: The Source of Ælfric's Latin-Old English Grammar*, ed. David W. Porter (Cambridge, 2002); for a review article, see Gneuss, "The First Edition of the Source of Ælfric's *Grammar*," *Anglia*, 123 (2005), 244–59. It seems worth noting that the first scholar who recognized the relationship between the *Excerptiones* and Ælfric's work was not Max Förster but Julius Zupitza, who reported about this in 1887; see *Archiv für das Studium der Neueren Sprachen und Literaturen*, 79 (1887), 89.

day, with its own forms and categories. He recognized the common, basic structure of the two languages.

The instructional nature of the *Grammar* may also be seen from its appendix, namely a class-glossary consisting of more than 1,200 entries, which follows the *Grammar* in seven complete copies of the latter work. This so-called *Glossary* was designed to serve as a kind of basic dictionary for students of monastic schools.[60] A separate work by Ælfric, his *Colloquium,* a conversational manual of Latin intended for the same monastic students, reveals his ability to combine the role of the scholar with the practical needs of the teacher.[61] In any case, it is not impossible that the *Grammar* and *Glossary* may have been intended to contribute to the spread and establishment of Standard Old English.

---

60. Edited by by Julius Zupitza, *Grammatik,* pp. 297–322. For other editions and relevant bibliography, see Reinsma, no. 559 and pp. 183–90, as well as Gneuss, introduction to *Grammatik.* See now also Werner Hüllen, *English Dictionaries 800–1700: The Topical Tradition* (Oxford, 1990), pp. 62–66 and 451–52.

61. *Ælfrics's Colloquy,* ed. Garmonsway (cited above, n. 22); the Old English interlinear glossing in MS. Cotton Tiberius A. iii is not by Ælfric. On the abundant scholarly literature see Reinsma, pp. 167–75, as well as Patrizia Lendinara, "The *Colloquy* of Ælfric and the *Colloquy* of Ælfric Bata," in *Anglo-Saxon Glosses and Glossaries* (Aldershot, 1999), pp. 207–88; on the reworking of Ælfric's *Colloquium* by Ælfric Bata (probably a student of Ælfric), and on Ælfric Bata's own colloquies, see *Anglo-Saxon Conversations: The Colloquies of Ælfric Bata,* ed. Scott Gwara, with translations and introduction by David W. Porter (Woodbridge, 1997). The various sociological interpretations of Ælfric's *Colloquium*—which is, after all, an instructional manual—should be treated with skepticism; cf. however John Ruffing, "The Labor Structure of Ælfric's Colloquy," in *The Work of Work,* ed. Allen Frantzen and Douglas Moffat (Glasgow, 1994), pp. 55–70.

ANGLO-SAXON LITERATURE IN THE VERNACULAR

At this point it might seem appropriate to raise the question of why it was particularly in late Anglo-Saxon England that so abundant a prose literature in the vernacular should have developed, not merely in the domain of theological writings, while at the same time the older poetry was being copied and preserved. After King Alfred, Ælfric of Eynsham was the principal representative of that prose literature. Tradition and the formation of a national identity could be one answer. Another could be the necessity (caused by the decline of education in the ninth century and continuing deficiencies in the tenth, especially among the clergy—to which Ælfric himself draws attention) of providing English versions of essential texts, such as the Benedictine Rule, as a temporary remedy.[62]

The second answer represents the opinions that have been expressed by many distinguished scholars of the twentieth century, and these opinions are to some extent justified. It is possible here only to sketch out the arguments briefly. There are two arguments in particular: imperfect knowledge of Latin or no knowledge at all, and lacunose library holdings, especially in the field of patristic literature.[63] It is certain that the refoundation or reform of English monasteries continued throughout the tenth century, and that the Latin competence of the clergy only gradually improved. We are, however, able to evaluate the quality of the Latinity and the Latin learning of authors and scribes, and this quality often meets acceptable standards. As a counterargument to this optimistic view the liturgical scholar Christopher

---

62. On the situation in the ninth and early tenth century, see Helmut Gneuss, "Anglo-Saxon Libraries from the Conversion to the Benedictine Reform," in *Books and Libraries in Early England*, no. II, pp. 672–79, and "King Alfred and the History of Anglo-Saxon Libraries," ibid., no. III; Michael Lapidge, "Schools, Learning and Literature in Tenth-Century England," in *Anglo-Latin Literature 900–1066*, pp. 1–48 and 469, and idem, *Library*, pp. 44–50.

63. On the arguments of T. A. M. Bishop, Julian Brown, and Neil Ker, see Gneuss, "Anglo-Saxon Libraries" (cited above, n. 62), pp. 680–83; their arguments are advanced even more vigorously by Rodney M. Thomson, "The Norman Conquest and English Libraries," in *The Role of the Book in Medieval Culture*, ed. Peter Ganz (Turnhout, 1986), II. 27–40. The situation is viewed more realistically, and certainly more correctly, by Teresa Webber, "The Patristic Content of English Book Collections in the Eleventh Century: Towards a Continental Perspective," in *Of the Making of Books: Medieval Manuscripts, Their Scribes and Readers: Essays Presented to M. B. Parkes*, ed. P. R. Robinson and Rivkah Zim (Aldershot, 1997), pp. 191–205, and see now the important discussion and inventory in Lapidge, *Library*, pp. 69–70 and 275–342.

Hohler drew attention to the drinking habits of Anglo-Saxon monasteries; and in fact a chronicler—but one writing in the thirteenth century—cited the vast daily beer-ration which Æthelwold is said to have fixed for his monks in Abingdon, a ration which even devotees of the Munich Oktoberfest would regard with astonishment![64]

Nevertheless Old English prose literature should not be seen simply as providing substitutes for Latin originals. It is sufficient to draw attention here to the original texts which were composed in English, such as the Anglo-Saxon Chronicle and particularly the laws of Anglo-Saxon kings, conceived from the outset in the vernacular.[65]

What is not in doubt, as we now realize, are the demonstrable limitations in the holdings of libraries in monasteries and cathedral churches. The majority of what was still available in the ninth century was destroyed during the Danish wars of that century. The importation of books from Francia and intensive scriptorial activity, with a focus on the most important and indispensable texts, helped to create new and refurbished library collections. But this activity did not alleviate all the problems, and gaps still remained in library holdings. We can see what was rare or lacking in Anglo-Saxon collections by studying the Norman restocking of libraries from the late eleventh century onwards, as it can be traced in the surviving holdings of Canterbury, Rochester, Salisbury, Exeter, and Durham, notably in those books containing patristic writings or school-texts (of the most widely read Roman poets) which were copied or imported at that time, texts which previously were extremely rare, or were lacking altogether.[66]

---

64. C. E. Hohler, "Some Service-Books of the Later Saxon Church," in *Tenth-Century Studies: Essays in Commemoration of the Millennium of the Council of Winchester and Regularis Concordia*, ed. David Parsons (London, 1975), pp. 61–83; on the so-called *bolla Æthelwoldi*, see p. 71 and accompanying notes, as well as Knowles, *The Monastic Order in England*, Appendix XX.

65. Work continued on both Chronicle and laws during Ælfric's lifetime. On the remarkable use of the English vernacular for the composition of Anglo-Saxon law-codes from the very earliest times onwards, see now Patrick Wormald, *The Making of English Law: King Alfred to the Twelfth Century*, I: *Legislation and Its Limits* (Oxford, 1999), passim.

66. On the imports, and on English book production in the tenth and eleventh centuries, cf. Gneuss, *Handlist* (cited above, n. 2), and Lapidge, *Library*, esp. pp. 167–73. The Norman program of library restocking can be traced in the excellent synopsis and inventory of Richard Gameson, *The Manuscripts of Early Norman England (c. 1066–1130)* (Oxford, 1999).

Ælfric as Adviser of the Episcopacy and Nobility

In his monumental work on the monastic orders in England from the middle of the tenth century until the beginning of the thirteenth, Dom David Knowles singled out as one of the features which link Ælfric to his great predecessor in the north, Bede:[67] "the quiet life within the walls of a monastery." This is certainly true for Bede, and, at first glance, also for the learned homilist and grammarian Ælfric. Ælfric was clearly not a personality of public life; he was no episcopal dignitary (which explains why we lack a biography of him), and it seems unlikely, to judge from the witness-lists of Anglo-Saxon royal charters, that even as abbot he participated in the king's council, unlike other contemporaries of similar rank.[68] However, a careful reading of his writings indicates that long before his promotion to the abbacy (of Eynsham) Ælfric had assumed a role and enjoyed a prestige which must have seemed completely unusual for a cloistered monk. During a politically unstable period, he was willing to take on the tasks with which he was commissioned by the church and the nobility; he had the knowledge and the capacity to do so, and he was undoubtedly aware that such responsibilities had to lead him well away from the "quiet life" of the monastic community. In order to do justice to his achievements and influence, it would be necessary to provide a survey of the circumstances and development of the English state and church at the turn of the millennium, which is scarcely possible here.

But a significant fact deserves mention. From the tenth century until the Reformation a characteristic and distinctive feature of the English church was the institution of the monastic cathedral, which began with Æthelwold's expulsion of clerics from the Old Minster in Winchester in 964.[69] Already in

---

67. Knowles, *The Monastic Order in England*, pp. 61–64, 493–94.

68. This can clearly be seen from Simon Keynes, *An Atlas of Attestations in Anglo-Saxon Charters c. 670–1066*, I. *Tables*, ASNC Guides, Texts, and Studies 5 (Cambridge, 2002). The author kindly made available to me an earlier, privately printed version. See also Simon Keynes, *The Diplomas of King Æthelred 'the Unready' 978–1016: A Study in Their Use as Historical Evidence* (Cambridge, 1980), pp. 156–57, as well as Dorothy Whitelock, "The Date of Ælfric's Death" ("Two Notes on Ælfric and Wulfstan," in *History, Law and Literature in 10th–11th Century England* [London, 1981], no. X). On the problem of Anglo-Saxon name-giving, see above, n. 6.

69. Michael Lapidge in *Vita Æthelwoldi*, pp. xlv–li; Knowles, *The Monastic Order in England*, ch. XXXVI.

the tenth century Sherborne and possibly Canterbury and Worcester had become monastic cathedrals, and others, but not all, followed suit in the late eleventh and early twelfth century (Rochester, Durham, Bath, Norwich, Coventry, Ely). Ælfric had spent formative years, indeed decades, in such a monastic cathedral in Winchester, where the concerns of the diocese must also have been familiar to the monastic community; and his experiences there, as well as the deficiencies of the secular clergy at that time, must to some extent have occasioned the composition of the *Catholic Homilies*, as well as his preoccupation with canon law. His competence in this domain must have been well known, and is reflected in the fact that he was asked to compose the Pastoral Letters, that is to say, letters of exhortation to be sent by bishops not to their congregations but to the priests of their dioceses, in which the manner of living and the duties of priests were addressed in detail.[70]

Ælfric composed five such Pastoral Letters; namely one in English for Bishop Wulfsige of Sherborne (ca. 993–1002), then—again at the express request, this time of Archbishop Wulfstan of York (1002–23, and bishop of Worcester 1002–16)—two in Latin, which, again at Wulfstan's request, were later reworked, expanded, and translated into Old English. It is significant that even the great archbishop, himself a powerful preacher and author of secular and ecclesiastical laws, should have turned to Ælfric with this request—he must have had good reasons for doing so—just as Ælfric for his part submitted *his* homily collections, intended for the secular clergy, to his own archbishop, Sigeric in Canterbury (990–94), for approval.[71]

---

70. Complete edition by Bernhard Fehr, *Die Hirtenbriefe Ælfrics in altenglischer und lateinischer Fassung*. In the reprint (Darmstadt, 1966) Fehr's extensive introduction was supplied with a supplement by Peter Clemoes. Letters I, II, and 2a were also edited (and I and II provided with English translation) by Dorothy Whitelock in *Councils and Synods with Other Documents relating to the English Church I: A.D. 871–1204. Part I: 871–1066*, ed. Dorothy Whitelock, M. Brett, and C. N. L. Brooke (Oxford, 1981). On the content and circulation of the Letters: Joyce Hill, "Monastic Reform and the Secular Church: Ælfric's Pastoral Letters in Context," in *England in the Eleventh Century: Proceedings of the 1990 Harlaxton Symposium*, ed. Carola Hicks (Stamford, 1992), pp. 103–17.

71. On Wulfstan, see the bibliography listed by Andy Orchard, "Wulfstan," in *Blackwell Encyclopaedia*, pp. 494–95, and esp. Malcolm Godden, "The Relations of Wulfstan and Ælfric: A Reassessment," in *Wulfstan, Archbishop of York: The Proceedings of the Second Alcuin Conference*, ed. Matthew Townend (Turnhout, 2004), pp. 353–74. On Wulfstan's involvement in ecclesiastical legislation, see now Wormald, *The Making of English Law*, I, and *Wulfstan's Canon Law Collection*, ed. Cross and Hamer (cited above, n. 34), as well as Hans Sauer, "The Transmission and Structure of Archbishop Wulfstan's 'Commonplace Book,'" in *Old English Prose* (cited above, n. 1), pp. 339–93 (originally published in German in *Deutsches Archiv für Erforschung des Mittelalters* 36, 1980).—Ælfric's prefaces to Sigeric: *Catholic Homilies* I. 173–74 and II. 1; English translations in Wilcox, *Prefaces*, pp. 127–29.

As with bishops, so Ælfric cultivated contacts with influential laymen, who consulted him for advice and guidance, and to whom he lent books. From the period of his abbacy at Eynsham the following are known by name (but are not always securely identifiable): Sigefyrth, and Wulfgeat "æt Yl-mandune"; also Sigeweard "æt Eastheolon," for whom Ælfric composed his summary of the Bible. These men were landowning nobles of the rank of *thegn*, and Ælfric had personal dealings with all of them. For example, he reproves Sigeweard because at a get-together he had pressed Ælfric to drink more than was customary or manageable for him.[72]

Two distinguished noblemen, who had greatly esteemed Ælfric over a long period and who helped in his personal advancement, were Æthel-weard, the *ealdorman* of southwest England, and his son Æthelmær, who also subsequently became *ealdorman* in the Southwest. Both had literary interests and both read Ælfric's writings, or even occasioned their composition. Æthelweard, who ranked among the greatest of the nobles and was himself of royal lineage, was the author of a Latin translation of the *Anglo-Saxon Chronicle* (his translation carries a dedication to Abbess Matilda of Essen, a granddaughter of Emperor Otto I and his Anglo-Saxon wife Eadgyth), which has independent value as a historical source, and is notorious for its hermeneutic Latin (which *inter alia* was not prized by William of Malmes-bury). His son Æthelmær was the founder of the abbey of Cerne (Ælfric was sent, or at least seconded, there at Æthelmær's request) and the abbey of Eynsham, to the northwest of Oxford, owes its establishment to Æthelmær as well.[73]

---

72. On Sigefyrth: *Angelsächsische Homilien und Heiligenleben*, ed. Bruno Assmann, p. 13, as well as Clemoes in his supplement, pp. xvi–xix; Assmann, pp. 246–49; and on Ælfric's polemic against clerical marriage in the *Letter to Sigefyrth*, see Jonathan Wilcox, "The Transmission of Ælfric's *Letter to Sigefyrth* and the Mutilation of MS Cotton Vespasian D. xiv," in *Early Medieval English Texts and Interpretations* (cited above, n. 9), pp. 285–300.—Wulfgeat: Assmann, pp. 1–12, 243–46 as well as Clemoes, pp. xi–xvi.—Sigeweard: *Heptateuch*, pp. 15–16, 74–75. On the uncertain identification of these three men, see Keynes, *The Diplomas of King Æthelred 'the Unready' 978–1016*, p. 193 n. 143. For another interesting exhortative message by Ælfric, see now Mary Clayton, "An Edition of Ælfric's *Letter to Brother Edward*," in *Early Medieval English Texts and Interpretations*, pp. 263–83.

73. On Æthelweard: Ælfric, *Heptateuch*, pp. 76–80; *Lives of Saints*, I. 4–6; Sean Miller, "Æthelweard," in *Blackwell Encyclopaedia*, p. 18; Keynes, *Diplomas of King Æthelred*, pp. 191–92 and passim. On Æthelmær, see now the thorough discussion in Jones, *Eynsham Letter*, pp. 6–16. On the historical background, see below, n. 77, as well as Simon Keynes, "Apocalypse Then: England A.D. 1000," in *Europe around the Year 1000*, ed. Przemyslaw Urbánczyk (Warsaw, 2001), pp. 247–70.

The Royal House and the Scandinavian Wars

From the brief sketch presented hitherto, it will be clear that Ælfric was able to enjoy the "quiet life within the walls of a monastery" only to a limited degree, but that his activities—prompted by the sense of his Christian calling and of his role as a promoter of learning—had an impact on church and laity beyond his immediate surroundings in Wessex and Mercia. Limits at any rate were set for him, or else he set them for himself: his connection with the royal court of Æthelred, who reigned since 978, appears to have been tenuous. His ideal of kingship was focused on Æthelred's predecessors, who had freed the country from the menace and domination of the Vikings: Alfred (871–99) and Æthelstan (924–39); but this ideal was above all embodied in Edgar (959–75), who had maintained the peace in England and had given decisive support to the monastic reforms of Dunstan, Æthelwold, and Oswald.[74]

One of the principal features of the monastic reform is the close connection between the monasteries and their royal protectors. This connection is fully documented in the *Regularis Concordia*. (This customary was issued, following a synod in Winchester in about 973, by way of supplement to the Benedictine Rule; its intention was to put monastic life in England, particularly its liturgical use, on a common footing.)[75] In his adaptation of the *Concordia* for the monks of Eynsham, it seems that Ælfric deliberately allowed the connection between monasteries and the royal house to slip into the background. The *Regularis Concordia* had been specifically concerned with consolidating the authority of the crown and with eliminating the claims of ownership and of control exercised by the nobility—the *saecularium prioratus*—over monasteries. But circumstances had changed. Ælfric

---

74. Ælfric, *Heptateuch*, pp. 416–17, as well as in his Life of St. Swithun, *Lives of Saints*, I. 468, lines 444–53. Skeat's edition of this Life has now been superseded by the definitive critical and annotated edition in Michael Lapidge, *The Cult of St. Swithun*, Winchester Studies 4.ii (Oxford, 2003), pp. 575–609; for the cited passage, see p. 606, lines 234–39.

75. Edition, including interlinear glosses, with extensive introduction and annotation: *Die Regularis Concordia und ihre altenglische Interlinearversion*, ed. Lucia Kornexl, TUEPh 17 (Munich, 1993); edition with English translation: *Regularis Concordia Anglicae Nationis Monachorum Sanctimonialiumque*, ed. Thomas Symons (London, 1953); cf. also the text edited by Symons and Sigrid Spath in the *Corpus Consuetudinum Monasticarum* VII/3 (Siegburg, 1984). On the historical background, see Kornexl, pp. xvi–lvi, and also above, n. 64.

saw monastic life in southwest England, and hence his aims and influence, being directly supported by the nobility. Moreover, the reign of Æthelred bore no comparison with Edgar's peaceful reign; indeed, King Æthelred, at least in his early years, was himself involved in the curtailment of rights and the appropriation of lands of a number of churches and monasteries.[76]

Æthelred "the Unready" (that is, "lacking counsel"), as he was later called, has for centuries been seen by historians in very unkindly terms. Only in our own times has it become possible to form a more unbiased and not entirely negative judgment of him. It was his and England's misfortune that his reign fell during the period of the Second Viking Age, which ultimately resulted in the victory of the Danish kings Swein and Knut over the Anglo-Saxons.[77]

For more than three decades, beginning in 980, England for the second time was being attacked by Scandinavians in piratical raids and military expeditions. It is precisely the period in which Ælfric's life as monk, priest, and abbot, and the composition of all his writings, took place, and in which the monasteries in the southwest of the country were also affected by the events of the war. Ælfric repeatedly refers to this situation, beginning with the Latin preface to the Second Series of *Catholic Homilies*, which he had prepared *dolente animo*, in spite of the atrocities perpetrated by the hostile sea-raiders (*multis iniuriis infestium piratarum*). Later he was to see in the hunger, epidemics, and Viking attacks a divine punishment for the persecution—the so-called anti-monastic reaction—which English monasteries had suffered after the death of King Edgar. Finally, however, his condemnation and anger turned on the Vikings themselves: they were the instruments of the devil; plunder and murder were second nature to them, as they had already demonstrated when they killed the East Anglian king Eadmund (St. Edmund, 869), whose martyrdom Ælfric described in his *Lives of Saints*, basing himself on Abbo of Fleury. Therefore we are fighting a "just war" (*iustum bellum*), against the Vikings; the Old Testament offers as models

76. On Ælfric's attitude towards King Æthelred, and the underlying reasons: Jones in *Eynsham Letter*, pp. 42–49, and Mary Clayton, "Ælfric and Æthelred," in *Essays on Anglo-Saxon and Related Themes in Memory of Lynne Grundy*, ed. Jane Roberts and Janet Nelson, King's College London Medieval Studies XVII (London, 2000), pp. 65–88, as well as Keynes, *Diplomas of King Æthelred*, pp. 176–86.

77. Simon Keynes, "The Declining Reputation of Æthelred the Unready," in *Anglo-Saxon History: Basic Readings*, ed. David A. E. Pelteret (New York, 2000), pp. 157–90 (first published 1978); idem, "The Historical Context of the Battle of Maldon," in *The Battle of Maldon AD 991* (cited above, n. 56), pp. 81–113.

Judith and the Maccabees; in my own manner I have turned the book of Judith into English (that is, as a homily), "as an example for you Englishmen, that you should defend your homeland with weapons against the attacking enemy army."[78]

The Scandinavian invasions must also have seemed to Ælfric a sign of the approaching end of the world. Apocalypse and the concept of the ages of the world are recurrent themes of his homilies, themes which obviously lay close to his heart. In the Sixth Age the present world will come to its end, with the advent of the Antichrist, with the resurrection of the dead, and the final judgment. Ælfric perceived these events as imminent, but: no one knows the exact hour. Accordingly, there is no indication anywhere in his writings that the last age of the world was to end precisely in the year 1000.[79]

78. The quotation is from *Heptateuch*, p. 48.—Ælfric's attitude to, and treatment of, the Scandinavian invasions are discussed by Malcolm Godden, "Ælfric's Saints Lives and the Problem of Miracles," in *Sources and Relations: Studies in Honour of J. E. Cross*, ed. Marie Collins, Jocelyn Price, and Andrew Hamer, *Leeds Studies in English* n.s. 16 (Leeds, 1985), pp. 83–100, as well as idem, "Apocalypse and Invasion in Late Anglo-Saxon England," in *From Anglo-Saxon to Early Middle English: Studies Presented to E. G. Stanley*, ed. Malcolm Godden, Douglas Gray, and Terry Hoad (Oxford, 1994), pp. 130–62; and see now Simon Keynes, "An Abbot, an Archbishop, and the Viking Raids of 1006–7 and 1009–12," *ASE*, 36 (2007), 151–220, at 160–70. On the *iustum bellum*, see J. E. Cross, "The Ethic of War in Old English," in *England before the Conquest: Studies in Primary Sources Presented to Dorothy Whitelock*, ed. Peter Clemoes and Kathleen Hughes (Cambridge, 1971), pp. 269–82. On the historical background, see also above, n. 77. Another example of Ælfric's position on royal deeds and misdeeds—in this case the St. Brice's Day massacre of the Danes in England in 1002—is suggested by Mary Clayton, "Ælfric's *Esther: A Speculum Reginae?*" in *Text and Gloss: Studies in Insular Learning and Literature Presented to Joseph Donovan Pheifer*, ed. Helen Conrad O'Briain et al. (Dublin, 1999), pp. 89–101.

79. On the millennium, the ages of the world, and the expectation of the end: Dorothy Bethurum, *The Homilies of Wulfstan* (Oxford, 1957), pp. 278–82; Milton McC. Gatch, *Preaching and Theology in Anglo-Saxon England* (cited above, n. 35), chs. 7 and 10; Joyce Hill, "Ælfric and Wulfstan: Two Views of the Millennium," in *Essays in Memory of Lynne Grundy* (cited above, n. 76), pp. 213–35; Hildegard C. Tristram, *Sex aetates mundi. Die Weltzeitalter bei den Angelsachsen und Iren* (Heidelberg, 1985), on Ælfric passim. Cf. Keynes, *Bibliography*, pp. 154–55, J 37–39, and above, n. 73.

ART AND CULTURE IN WINCHESTER

We see Ælfric today as a theologian and philologist, as a teacher and coun-
selor, whose influence extended far beyond the walls of the monastery, but
we should not forget the immediate context in which he lived, learning and
teaching for more than two decades, and perhaps a good deal longer, and
which must have had a lasting impact on him. That immediate environment
was the Old Minster, the monastic cathedral in Winchester in the time of
Bishops Æthelwold (963–84) and Ælfheah (984–1006) and their students
and collaborators. No other institution in England exerted a comparable
influence, in learning and the arts, in the second half of the tenth century,
and even into the eleventh.[80]

Ælfric was naturally familiar with Winchester's library holdings and
book production. He doubtless knew the important role which the Old
Minster had played in the introduction of Caroline minuscule script in
England and had surely seen one of the most perfect examples of that
script, perhaps already at the time of its production (971×984), namely the
Benedictional of St Æthelwold, which was written and provided with a Latin
dedicatory poem in hexameters by his monastic confrere Godeman and
which, because of its decoration and its underlying iconographic program,
must be regarded as the most significant example of late Anglo-Saxon book
production and the masterpiece of the Winchester School in the time of
Æthelwold and Ælfric.[81]

---

80. See above all Lapidge, in the introduction to *Vita Æthelwoldi; Bishop Æthelwold*, ed.
Yorke (cited above, n. 11), especially the article by Lapidge, "Æthelwold as Scholar and Teach-
er," reprinted with "Additional Notes" in *Anglo-Latin Literature 900–1066*, pp. 183–211 and 482;
Gretsch, *The Intellectual Foundations of the English Benedictine Reform*.

81. On the role of Winchester in the history of script, see T. A. M. Bishop, *English Caro-
line Minuscule* (Oxford, 1971); David N. Dumville, *English Caroline Script and Monastic History:
Studies in Benedictinism, A.D. 950–1030* (Woodbridge, 1993); on manuscript art of the period,
Elzbieta Temple, *Anglo-Saxon Manuscripts 900–1066: A Survey of Manuscripts Illuminated in the
British Isles* II (London, 1976); Thomas H. Ohlgren, *Insular and Anglo-Saxon Illuminated Manu-
scripts: An Iconographic Catalogue c. A.D. 625 to 1100* (New York, 1986); Robert Deshman, *The
Benedictional of Æthelwold* (Princeton, NJ, 1995), with a complete color facsimile now available
as *The Benedictional of St. Æthelwold: A Masterpiece of Anglo-Saxon Art*, intro. Andrew Prescott
(London, 2002). For extensive coverage of the art of the period, see the excellent exhibition
catalogue, *The Golden Age of Anglo-Saxon Art 966–1066*, ed. Janet Backhouse, D. H. Turner, and
Leslie Webster (London, 1984); and see also Richard Gameson, *The Role of Art in the Late Anglo-
Saxon Church* (Oxford, 1995).

A particularly important witness to what was being achieved at the Old Minster during Ælfric's lifetime is the work of another confrere, likewise a student of Æthelwold, namely Wulfstan Cantor (not to be confused with later bishops of the same name), whose importance has only been properly appreciated in recent times. Wulfstan was active as a poet and composer; he was perhaps one of the scribes of the earliest manuscript of the Winchester Troper (MS. Corpus Christi College, Cambridge, 473), which contains a number of tropes and sequences composed by him. Similarly a number of hymns for Winchester saints and other liturgical pieces can confidently be ascribed to him.[82] Wulfstan doubtless owed his schooling to Æthelwold, of whom he expressly states that he had learned not only the *ars* of grammar but also the *mellifluam metricae rationis dulcedinem* ("the honey-sweet system of metrics") in Glastonbury, and that he subsequently taught both these disciplines in Winchester. It is therefore not a matter of chance that we find among the writings of Wulfstan a hymn in sapphic stanzas, and even a hymn in the second asclepiadeic stanza is probably to be ascribed to him as well.[83] Interestingly, Ælfric notes in the Latin preface to his *Grammar* that, for didactic reasons, he unfortunately cannot deal with the subject of metrics (a subject with which he was obviously familiar).

It is clear that Winchester in Ælfric's lifetime was also the leading center of English musical life, at least in the domain of liturgical music. We find here, in the manuscript of the Winchester Troper just mentioned, the earliest repertory of polyphonic Organa (*melliflua organorum modulamina*), composed to accompany mass-chants, which has been preserved in England or Europe, and the composition of the majority of these Organa is now ascribed to Wulfstan Cantor. It should also be noted that the Winchester Troper, as well as the Winchester-produced *Regularis Concordia*, are witnesses to the Easter trope *Quem quaeritis*, which has long been seen as the seed from which medieval drama grew.[84] To Wulfstan we owe further evidence for the history of English music, namely, his account of the famous organ in the Old Minster, a massive instrument consisting of four hundred pipes

---

82. On the life and writings of Wulfstan of Winchester, see now the authoritative treatment by Michael Lapidge in the introduction to Wulfstan's *Vita Æthelwoldi*, pp. xiii–xxxix and passim.

83. On the hymns, see Dieter Schaller and Ewald Könsgen, *Initia carminum Latinorum saeculo undecimo antiquiorum* (Göttingen, 1977), nos. 8011 (sapphic stanzas) and 1558 (second asclepiadeic stanzas); cf. Lapidge, *Vita Æthelwoldi*, pp. xxv and xxxvii; the second hymn has recently been edited as no. 85 in Inge B. Milfull, *The Hymns of the Anglo-Saxon Church*, CSASE 17 (Cambridge, 1996).

84. On the tropes and Organa in the Winchester Tropers: Alejandro Enrique Planchart, *The Repertory of Tropes at Winchester*, 2 vols. (Princeton, NJ, 1977); Andreas Holschneider, *Die*

which was played by two monks at individual manuals, and which could be heard through the entire city and was famous throughout the entire country:

> Musarumque melos auditur ubique per urbem
> et peragrat totam fama uolans patriam.[85]

Finally, mention should be made of the fact that Wulfstan of Winchester also composed a work on musical theory, the *Breviloquium super musicam*, which has probably been lost (or at least remains to be discovered and identified).[86]

The description of the organ in Winchester is contained in the *Epistola specialis* addressed to Bishop Ælfheah, which serves as a preface to Wulfstan's *Narratio metrica de S. Swithuno*, completed in 996 and made up of more than 3,000 hexameters, on the translation and miracles of Bishop Swithun of Winchester (852×853–862×865), and which is another outstanding witness to Wulfstan's metrical skill. The *Epistola specialis* contains descriptions of two ceremonies of dedication at the Old Minster, the first in 980, the second 992×994. Ælfric will have participated in the first of these at least, and will also have witnessed the occasion for these ceremonies, likewise described in detail by Wulfstan, namely the building activities which led to the reconstruction and extension of the cathedral (which up until the tenth century had been a far from imposing structure) under Æthelwold and Ælfheah, with its crypts, side-chapels, west-work, and tower surmounted by a golden

---

Organa von Winchester (Hildesheim, 1968); Susan Rankin, "Winchester Polyphony: The Early Theory and Practice of Organon," in *Music in the Medieval English Liturgy*, ed. Susan Rankin and David Hiley (Oxford, 1993), pp. 59–99, and Rankin, *The Winchester Troper*. Facsimile edition and introduction, Early English Church Music 50 (London, 2008). Two recordings by the Schola Gregoriana in Cambridge, under the direction of Mary Berry, which are drawn from the Winchester Troper and reproduce some of the Organa, have been made: 1. *Anglo-Saxon Easter* (originally a vinyl record: Archiv 413546-1, 1984; a CD version was issued by the Past Times label, but appears no longer to be available); 2. *Christmas in Royal Anglo-Saxon Winchester* (CD: Herald HAVPC 151, 1992). On the *Quem quaeritis*: see now Kornexl, *Die Regularis Concordia* (cited above, n. 75), p. lxviii and n. 54, and Peter Williams (below, n. 85), pp. 88–89, with bibliography.

85. On the organ: Wulfstan, *Narratio metrica de S. Swithuno*, ed. Lapidge, *The Cult of St. Swithun*, pp. 382–86, "Epistola specialis," lines 145–76, with excellent commentary (the quotation is from lines 173–74). On Wulfstan's writings, see Lapidge in *Vita Æthelwoldi*, pp. xx–xxii. For discussion of the Winchester organ, see also Peter Williams, *The Organ in Western Culture 750–1250* (Cambridge, 1993), pp. 123–34, 187–203, and passim; on the terminology, see Gretsch, *The Intellectual Foundations of the English Benedictine Reform*, pp. 394–96.

86. See Lapidge in *Vita Æthelwoldi*, pp. xvi–xvii.

weathercock.[87] Wulfstan's description of the building as it existed in his lifetime is unfortunately rather vague in architectural detail, but his enthusiastic account was nevertheless brilliantly confirmed a thousand years later by Martin Biddle, who during the years 1961–71 excavated the foundations of the Anglo-Saxon Old Minster. The excavations revealed that the Old Minster was without doubt the most imposing ecclesiastical structure of the Anglo-Saxon period, and it is the only large cathedral building of this period to have been fully revealed in this way, the revelation being facilitated by the slightly different east-west orientation of the old (Anglo-Saxon) cathedral, and the new (Norman) cathedral which replaced it, which allowed the excavators direct access to the foundations of the former.[88]

87. Ed. Lapidge, *The Cult of St. Swithun*, pp. 374–76 and 380–82, "Epistola specialis," lines 35–60, 115–44, with detailed commentary. I am deeply grateful to Professor Lapidge for providing me with typescript copies of relevant parts of his edition before it was published.

88. Martin Biddle, *"Felix urbs Winthonia*: Winchester in the Age of Monastic Reform," in *Anglo-Saxon History* (cited above, n. 77), pp. 289–316, first published 1975; idem, "The Study of Winchester: Archaeology and History in a British Town, 1961–1983," *Proceedings of the British Academy*, 69 (1983), 93–135, with bibliography of all relevant publications, including the "Interim Reports" on the excavations, 1961–75. The final report is forthcoming: Martin Biddle and Birthe Kjølbye Biddle, *The Anglo-Saxon Minsters of Winchester*, Winchester Studies 4.i. See also H. M. Taylor and Joan Taylor, *Anglo-Saxon Architecture*, III (Cambridge, 1978), 743–45. Hypothetical reconstructions of the Old Minster may be seen in *Blackwell Encyclopaedia*, p. 481, and in Martin Biddle, "Archaeology, Architecture and the Cult of Saints in Anglo-Saxon England," in *The Anglo-Saxon Church: Papers on History, Architecture and Archaeology in Honour of Dr H. M. Taylor*, ed. L. A. S. Butler and R. K. Morris (London, 1986), pp. 1–31.

The Survival of Ælfric's Writings

Ælfric's writings, especially his homilies and the *Grammar*, were still being read, copied, and provided with glosses in the twelfth century.[89] In Worcester in the thirteenth century, a monk of the monastic cathedral occupied himself with the writings, and it is possible that he meant to use Ælfric's homilies as material for the preparation of contemporary sermons. Following this there is a break, not because Ælfric's work had been superseded but because his language could no longer be understood.[90]

In the sixteenth century Ælfric's writings came back to life: they were read, and were still found useful. They were used, for example, by the leading lights of the reformed English church, and above all by the antiquaries who now included works in Old English in their studies.[91] Following the Reformation, the attempt under Queen Mary (1553–58) to return to the Roman Catholic church failed. Her successor, Elizabeth I, appointed Protestant bishops, notably Matthew Parker as archbishop of Canterbury. His aim, and that of his circle, was to vindicate the reformed church (and its fundamental doctrines, as set out in the *Thirty-Nine Articles* of 1563) and to represent it not as a church of innovation and upheaval but rather as an institution that had restored true and ancient beliefs. The new church, in other words, was in reality the ancient and legitimate church, and among its legitimate responsibilities was that of translating the Bible into the language of its believers (as Ælfric had done) in order to make it accessible to them. The West Saxon translation of the Gospels, which had been in circulation in England since the tenth century, and which was published in 1571 through Parker's recommendation, could be a useful witness to this concern, as the martyrologist John Foxe explained in the preface, dedicated to the queen, to that edition:

---

89. For the homilies, see *Rewriting Old English in the Twelfth Century*, ed. Mary Swan and Elaine M. Treharne, CSASE 30 (Cambridge, 2000); for twelfth-century Latin, English, and French glosses in copies of the *Grammar* and *Glossary*, see Tony Hunt, *Teaching and Learning Latin in Thirteenth-Century England* (Cambridge, 1991), I. 23–26 and 99–118.

90. See above, n. 27.

91. The ever-increasing interest in the antiquaries of the sixteenth to eighteenth centuries is documented in Keynes, *Bibliography*, pp. 262–73.

> Likewise haue we to vnderstand and conceaue, by the edition hereof, how
> the religion presently taught and professed in the Church at thys present,
> is no new reformation of thinges lately begonne, which were not before,
> but rather a reduction of the Church to the Pristine state of old confor-
> mitie, which once it had, and almost lost by discontinuance of a fewe later
> years.[92]

Five years earlier Parker had already effected the publication of a booklet
which touched on a fundamental aspect of Christian belief, namely, the
doctrine of the transubstantiation. The principal content of the booklet
is an Easter homily from the Second Series of Ælfric's *Catholic Homilies* (II
no. xv), alongside excerpts from three of his Pastoral Letters, all under the
title *A Testimonie of Antiquitie*.[93] In these texts, and most fully in the homily,
Ælfric explains that the change of bread and wine into the body and blood
of Christ is not to be understood *lichamlice*, physically or corporeally, but
gastlice, spiritualiter. Much has been written in recent times about this (not
wholly unambiguous) homily and its exegesis, which I cannot go into here.
Two points need to be made, however. The editors of the *Testimonie of Antiquitie* had read the crucial passages in the homily from their own point of
view and had interpreted them accordingly (in their own accompanying
translation). Secondly, there is no doubt that Ælfric's direct source for the
crucial part of his homily was not one of the homiliaries on which he nor-
mally drew but rather the treatise *De corpore et sanguine Domini* of Ratramnus
of Corbie, whose position on the question of the Eucharist was thoroughly
familiar to English theologians of the Reformation.[94]

For the theologians as well as for the antiquaries of the sixteenth and
seventeenth centuries, with historical and legal-historical interests, Old
English was in many ways a foreign language. The rapid disappearance of
the inflectional system and the increasing romanization of the vocabulary

---

92. *The Gospel of the fower Euangelistes translated in the olde Saxon tyme out of Latin into the
vulgare toung of the Saxons* (London, 1571), p. 9.

93. *A Testimonie of Antiquitie, shewing the auncient fayth in the Church of England touching the
sacrament of the body and bloude of the Lord, here publikely preached, and also receaued in the Saxons
tyme, aboue 600. yeares agoe* (London, 1566 or 1567).

94. On the sources and interpretation of Ælfric's *Catholic Homily* II no. xv, see now Godden in *Catholic Homilies* III. 487–500; Theodore H. Leinbaugh, "Ælfric's *Sermo de Sacrificio in Die
Pascae*: Anglican Polemic in the Sixteenth and Seventeenth Centuries," in *Anglo-Saxon Scholar-
ship: The First Three Centuries*, ed. Carl T. Berkhout and Milton McC. Gatch (Boston, 1982), pp.
51–68; and Lynne Grundy, "Ælfric's *Sermo de sacrificio in die Pascae: Figura* and *veritas*," *Notes and
Queries*, 235 (1990), 265–69. See also E. G. Stanley, "The Scholarly Recovery of the Significance
of Anglo-Saxon Records in Prose and Verse: A New Bibliography," ASE, 9 (1981), 223–62, esp.
229–30.

had altered the English language fundamentally. For the study of Old English these scholars had neither printed dictionaries nor grammar books. The earliest published grammar, by George Hickes, appeared only in 1689; the earliest dictionary, the *Dictionarium Saxonico-Latino-Anglicum* by William Somner, in 1659. This dictionary, apparently intended as a compendium of the Anglo-Saxon language, was supplemented by the author's inclusion of an edition of Ælfric's *Grammar*. The usefulness of the *Grammar*, together with the accompanying *Glossary*, even more than four hundred years after their composition, becomes clear from the numerous manuscript copies of the work which were made in the sixteenth and seventeenth centuries, and of which ten have been preserved to the present day.[95]

At the beginning of this lecture I described Ælfric (and thus his work) as a star which scarcely shines in the firmament of today's medievalists, whether in England or on the Continent. The situation may once have been different, and I should like to conclude by referring to two verses found in a manuscript which deserves much more thorough study. In the first twelve pages of MS. lat. 7561 of the Bibliothèque Nationale de France in Paris, which originally constituted a separate quire, there is a grammatical treatise (pp. 1–10), so far unidentified, which is followed by a Latin distich added at the top of the (originally blank) p. 12. The author of the distich expresses a wish on behalf of the monk Ælfric that "this work," which he composed for the honor and adornment of his church, may shine beyond the stars:

Ælfrico monacho opus hoc super astra coruscet
    Qui studuit templi sic decus hoc fieri.

The verses were manifestly copied by an Anglo-Saxon at some point in the eleventh century.[96] One would like to be able to link these verses to the preceding grammatical work, as the scribe apparently intended. But the work has no connection whatsoever with Ælfric's *Grammar*, in particular since it was copied in the late ninth century, as Bernhard Bischoff established, perhaps in France (Brittany?), perhaps by a continental scribe active

---

95. Cf. Gneuss in the introduction to *Grammatik*, pp. x–xii.

96. The verses (with the erroneous reading *Aelprico*) were printed by Manitius, *Geschichte der lateinischen Literatur des Mittelalters*, II. 680 n. 5, who considered it possible ("vielleicht") that the grammatical treatise on pp. 1–10 was by Ælfric himself. The verses are not listed by Schaller—Könsgen, *Initia* (cited above, n. 83), nor by Hans Walther, *Initia carminum et versuum Medii Aevi posterioris Latinorum*, 2nd ed. (Göttingen, 1969).

in England.[97] On the other hand, it seems certain to me that the later scribe of the distich—or at least its author—can only have been referring to Ælf- ric of Eynsham. Did the distich originate in a manuscript of the *Grammar*? But how and by what means it fetched up in the Paris manuscript remains unclear. And with this small puzzle I should like to bring the lecture to a close.

97. Birgit Ebersperger kindly helped with bibliographical problems and made available to me Bernhard Bischoff's notes, which will form the basis of the entry on BNF, lat. 7561 in the third volume of his *Katalog der festländischen Handschriften des neunten Jahrhunderts.*

INDEX OF SCHOLARS

This Index lists the names of scholars and editors whose writings and editions are cited either in the Abbreviated References or in the footnotes. Reference in each case is made only to the first and complete citation of an individual work. The numbers refer to the footnotes; Abb. = Abbreviated References (above, pp. ix–x).

Typeset in 10/13 ITC New Baskerville
Designed by Linda K. Judy
Composed by Linda K. Judy
Manufactured by McNaughton & Gunn, Inc.

Medieval Institute Publications
College of Arts and Sciences
Western Michigan University
1903 W. Michigan Avenue
Kalamazoo, MI 49008-5432
http://wmich.edu/medievalpublications

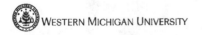
WESTERN MICHIGAN UNIVERSITY

9781580441445